Swen Nater is a spectacular human being. He brings so much to this world in the way of life wisdom and service to others, and now he has given us a book that helps us grow this wonderful game of basketball. This enjoyable read is also practical and full of insight. I highly recommend you take the time to absorb this strong teaching from one of our best Bruins.

Cori Close, Head Women's Basketball Coach, UCLA

Being a successful basketball coach for over three decades, I highly recommend Swen Nater's *Unstoppable: Developing a Great Basketball Post Player*. All basketball coaches and players should read this book. Swen shares the qualities and fundamentals needed to be an outstanding post player. A great post player himself, Swen details what he learned playing against some of the best post players in the history of the game, as well as what the great John Wooden taught him at UCLA. Take your game to a higher level by devouring the wisdom of this book!

Jim Johnson, Retired Head Boys Basketball Coach, Greece Athena High School (NY), Over 400 Career Wins

If you want to understand and learn how to play the game and then apply it to actual game improvement, then Swen Nater's *Unstoppable: Developing a Great Basketball Post Player* is a must-have. Throughout his career, Swen has learned from the best and now he is sharing the next level of the game for all post players. I will be buying his book for my son.

Nancy Lieberman, Naismith Memorial Basketball Hall of Famer, Second Female Assistant Coach in the NBA (Sacramento Kings)

If I were a martial artist, I would want to be taught by someone who trained under Bruce Lee. As a basketball coach, I want to be taught by someone who played for and learned from Coach John Wooden. Not only was Swen Nater an excellent player who learned to excel at the highest levels, he is the best basketball teacher I have ever met. For those of you who have ever said, "I wish I could go back to when basketball was fun," I'll say this, you *can*! Swen Nater makes you think, and he makes it fun. His understanding of and love for basketball, along with his competitive spirit and immense practical insights, are *beyond* rare. His ability to communicate them, even more so! I will certainly be putting the teachings in this terrific book into practice, and I greatly anticipate seeing the results in my players and teams as I do.

Patrick De Smet, Head Boys Basketball Coach, Issaquah (WA) High School

UNSTOPPABLE
Developing a Great Basketball Post Player

Swen Nater

COACHES ≡ CHOICE™

ISBN: 978-1-60679-417-3
Library of Congress Control Number: 2017963456
Cover design: Cheery Sugabo
Book layout: Cheery Sugabo
Front cover photo: ©Albert Pena/Cal Sport Media/ZUMA Press
Diagrams: Reggie Sugabo

Coaches Choice
P.O. Box 1828
Monterey, CA 93942
www.coacheschoice.com

Dedication

This book is eagerly dedicated to the two wonderful people and dear friends who are responsible for my start in basketball: Coach Tom Lubin and Coach Don Johnson.

Tom Lubin

In September of 1968, I walked onto the Cypress College (California) campus, not having played one minute of organized basketball. While I was eating lunch my first day, Tom Lubin, noticing my height, sent one of the players over to ask me if I was planning on trying out for the team. That player introduced me to Tom, who was the chemistry professor and assistant basketball coach. He took me to the court, where he learned that, although I was 6'9", I could not jump and touch the rim. He taught me the hook shot and worked with me every day. I made the team but sat the bench for most of the season.

The summer between my freshman and sophomore years, Tom drove me to the L.A. inner city courts every Saturday to help me become a basketball player. At first, I thought it was a cruel thing to do, as I basically got my tail kicked for a few weeks. But he kept taking me back and, in time, I was the one kicking tail. Thanks, Tom, and thanks to some of those players who helped me.

In my sophomore year, I became an All-American, was MVP of the league and my team, and earned a full scholarship to UCLA. Thank you, Tom. He's remained my best friend ever since.

Don Johnson

A consensus All-American at UCLA in 1952, as well as an all-conference honoree, Don Johnson is one of the greatest Bruins ever. At 6'3", he led the Bruins in rebounding and that became my main inspiration for becoming a rebounder.

When Tom Lubin introduced me to Coach Johnson, I sensed a love I had never experienced before. My own father and stepfather couldn't have cared less about me, but Coach Johnson really cared.

I was a terrible player my first year at Cypress, but Coach Johnson believed in me and continued to teach me, even though there was little improvement for months. With two games to go in my freshman season, Coach Johnson put me in a game when our starting center had four fouls. I didn't disappoint him.

He called John Wooden and asked if Cypress could play the UCLA freshman team at Pauley Pavilion the next season. Coach Wooden agreed. Again, I didn't disappoint Coach Johnson and we won the game. I had 35 points and 25 rebounds. This led to Coach Wooden recruiting me to be Bill Walton's backup, which directly resulted in my being selected in the first round of the NBA draft.

At the beginning of my sophomore year, when I was leading Cypress to victory and my name was in every paper, my stepfather told me to quit the team. The next morning I left home. Although I had three molars that were decayed down to almost nothing, my stepfather had not sent me to the dentist. Every night, I fell asleep in excruciating pain. When I left home, Don Johnson sent me to his dentist, who, free of charge, did thousands of dollars of work on my teeth. Thanks, Coach Johnson, for all the love you gave me. I will never be able to repay you, but I have tried.

Acknowledgments

No man is an island. Whatever knowledge of the post game I may have can by no means be credited solely to me. I was given a solid foundation at Cypress College, where I started playing organized basketball. That foundation was tested greatly at UCLA, where I was taught the post by John Wooden and played against the great Bill Walton every day in practice. That accumulated knowledge was tested again at the professional level against the best post players in the world. After retirement from the NBA, when I began teaching post play, I received much help in learning how to transfer my knowledge to students.

In particular, I would like to acknowledge the following people who contributed to this book in one way or another.

Wendy Ghiora

Wendy Ghiora, my talented and wonderful wife, helped me greatly, not only with grammar, content, and presentation, but also in field study. Using her extensive knowledge and experience as a high school English teacher, she reviewed, corrected, and augmented every chapter of this book, more than once.

She also contributed greatly during field study. Before even one chapter was written, Wendy and I traveled the country, conducting our "Play Post Like the Pros" clinics, where she coached me, often leaving her sideline seat to give me advice on proper instruction, pointed out any player needs I may have missed, and always reminded me to finish each session with "reflection," where players paired up and told each other the one or two things they had learned that they were going to apply going forward. Thank you, Wendy, for your invaluable help and consistent encouragement. I love you so.

Tom Lubin and Frank Lubin

Frank "Frankenstein" Lubin was a 6'7" UCLA All-American and the starting center on the first U.S. Olympic basketball team in 1936 (Berlin). In his time, he was the best center in the world. Tom Lubin is his nephew and was the assistant coach at Cypress College when I played there. Frank taught Tom how to play the post game. Tom passed that invaluable knowledge on to me, particularly the hook shot, which became my main offensive weapon. He worked with me almost every day in community college, and in the off-season, he drove me to the inner city of Los Angeles so I could, painfully, learn how to play this wonderful game. When I was writing this book, Tom, who volunteers as the big man coach at a local high school, arranged for me to work with his post players. Through teaching those players, I learned more of what works at that level. Thank you, Tom, for all you did to help me become an effective post player and the numerous things you have done for me since.

Don Johnson

I absolutely need to include my first coach, Don Johnson, who gave me my start in this great sport at Cypress College. If the criteria for being allowed to be on his roster had been experience and the ability to immediately help the team win, I would have had no business being a member of the Cypress Chargers. But Coach Johnson saw something in me and put me on the team, and I would never have penned this book if he had not done so. But make no mistake; Don Johnson also taught me post play and made sure my teammates passed me the basketball. Thank you, Coach Johnson, for believing in a tall, gangly, and inexperienced young man and giving me the opportunity to grow.

Don Johnson is the most successful community college men's basketball coach in California history. He did things very much like John Wooden. Those two were the only coaches I had before going pro. I thought all coaches were that good. Boy, was I disappointed! They were better than any professional coach I had.

John Wooden

Without my improvement at UCLA, I would not have become the player I was, which would mean I would most likely not have written this book.

John Wooden was rare in many ways. He was extremely organized, diligently and passionately committed to continuous improvement, a role model beyond reproach, a leader of the highest order, and a master teacher. He was also rare because he was a guard who knew how to coach the post player. He had to learn the subject when Lewis Alcindor became a student-athlete at UCLA. Bill Walton, Ralph Drollinger, and I reaped the benefits of his intense study of how to use the big man effectively, which included offensive post play he had never done himself.

It is very possible I would not have been an NBA first-round draft pick without Coach Wooden interceding. When the 1972 U.S. Olympic Committee decided not to have Bill Walton on the team because Bill insisted on not having to try out, which I completely agree with, Coach asked if they would allow me to be his replacement in the trials. They agreed and I led the entire tournament in scoring. This gave me instant national attention. When Bill Walton declined to play in the post-season Pizza Hut College All-Star Game in 1973, Coach asked if I could be his replacement. They agreed and I was MVP of the game. Thank you, Coach Wooden, for teaching me the post game and giving me opportunities to showcase my talents.

Jim Peterson and Kristi Huelsing (of Coaches Choice)

After *The Complete Handbook of Rebounding* (co-written with Jim Peterson), which did not sell nearly as well as we hoped, I'm surprised Jim Peterson, president of Coaches Choice, agreed to do another book with me. I am thankful for your faith in me, Jim. Kristi, thank you for coaching me along the way. Your advice and candid suggestions helped to keep me on task and on the path for a successful publication.

Paris Lubin-Gonsalves

I've known Paris since he was born. He is Tom Lubin's grandson. No one I have ever known loves the game of basketball more than he does. The poor defender you will see in the photos of this book is Paris. It was a hot day and I bumped him and leaned on him a lot. I'm 290 pounds and Paris is 180. The only reason he agreed to be part of this is because he loves the game and wants more people to learn the wonderful world of the inside game. Thanks, Paris. By the way, Paris Lubin-Gonsalves is a very good basketball player.

Foreword

At Power Memorial High School and UCLA, I was fortunate to have coaches who understood the post game and placed priority on the fundamentals. I truly believe that the solid foundation I received before I reached the NBA is largely responsible for my success on both ends of the floor.

This is why I am very pleased to see that Swen Nater has written a book on how to develop a great post player. Because I have seen many books on the subject through the years, I was initially skeptical as to how functional and useful it would be. Many of the publications I had read were very basic and rather conventional. What those writers taught certainly didn't fit with what I learned and did on the court. But Swen Nater has captured what it truly takes to be a post player. What he has written, you will find nowhere else.

When I saw his chapter on post moves, not only was I delighted he used my offensive game as an example, but I was pleasantly surprised Swen understood about a "two-move set." Contrary to what most coaches teach—a main move and a counter move—the counter move can be the main move if the defense calls for that. When I played in the NBA, I was always looking for my hook shot, but if the immediate drop step was available, I took it. That made me unpredictable.

Almost every chapter in this book has something like that in it, something that is not conventionally taught, but is true. Another example is, when sealing at the low post, a player should use the front pivot in order to make quicker and stronger contact and, equally important, to maintain vision on the ball. Most coaches teach the back pivot, which no one uses in the pros.

I respect Swen Nater as a person and a writer who is giving back to the game of basketball, and I always respected him as a player. I know his story. He didn't play in high school, but in five short years, he was playing in the ABA, and shortly thereafter, against me in the NBA. He gave me all I could handle.

When Swen Nater writes a book on post play, all coaches, especially at the high school level, should make it part of their libraries. He knows what he's talking about, because he actually did all of the things he writes about.

—Kareem Abdul-Jabbar

Contents

Introduction

I was born in Huisduinen, The Netherlands, on January 14, 1950. At age three, my mother and father divorced. They had three children: my older sister, Nanna (now Renee), me, and my little brother, Ibo. Because my mother, who had custody of all three children, could only afford to care for one of us, naturally, Ibo stayed with her while my sister and I moved in with a friend of hers. One and a half years later (1955), my mother, stepfather, and Ibo came for a visit. They announced we were being sponsored by a Quaker family and were going to America. That was the good news. The bad news was that the plan was for the three of them to go first, get established, and send for my sister and me when they raised the money. Four long years passed, and we were still in Holland. In the meantime, the two of us lived with three foster families and finally were moved to a home for children, something of an orphanage. I often wondered if I would ever see my mom again.

In late August of 1959, four years later, I found myself tucked in a miniature makeshift windmill with my sister, on an NBC stage, with the curtains closed. The nationally televised popular live Saturday evening television show *It Could Be You!* was about to begin, and my mother, my stepfather, and the sponsors were in the audience. Months before that day, the sponsors had approached the NBC show and presented the problem of a mother separated from two of her children. The show agreed to help, and just two days before the show, a KLM agent escorted my sister and me from the orphanage to the Beverly Hills Hotel. Talk about a huge change of environment! Meanwhile, the show gave the sponsors four tickets to the show. My mother and stepfather had no idea we were in town and a surprise reunion was about to occur. On live television, my parents were invited on stage. When the curtain was opened and they saw the windmill, the host asked, "Have you ever seen the inside of a windmill?" An usher opened the door, my sister and I raced out, and we were reunited with our family. We drove to Long Beach, California, where my parents and little brother lived.

One week after arriving in the United States, I was enrolled at Roosevelt Elementary School as a fourth grader, knowing no English. Ahead in math by one year, my teacher taught me how to read while the other students worked on math.

During recess and lunch, I mostly played kickball, where I excelled because of my extensive soccer experience in Holland. Tetherball and foursquare were also fun, but I had my eye on a game they called basketball. It was very much like soccer in the sense that there was teamwork and, to score, the ball was shot into a net. But it wasn't until middle school that I started to play the sport.

At Jefferson Middle School, still very slow afoot but with good hands and a nice touch with the jump shot (actually set shot because I couldn't jump very high), I played pick-up basketball at lunch and before school. I came to school one hour early just to get in some pick-up games.

At Woodrow Wilson High School, because of my love for the game, I continued my informal basketball experience, playing in gym class, at lunch, and after school. As a junior, I, the second-tallest kid in the school, tried out for the basketball team, only to be cut and asked not to try out again as a senior. You see, I tried out barefooted because my stepfather had not bought me tennis shoes yet. After two days of tryouts, Coach Bill Fraser said, "If you don't have a pair of shoes by tomorrow, don't bother coming back." When I was leaving the gym that day, I saw a pair of sneakers sitting in a corner, unattended, and decided I needed them more than the owner (whoever that was), so I took them. When I came to practice the next day, wearing size 13 Converse All Stars (I wore size 11), I saw the 6'6" starting center standing next to the coach, wearing only socks. So that's why I was cut and asked not to try out again the next year, and I don't blame the coach. Had I made the team, my stepfather would not have allowed me to play anyway.

After high school graduation, we moved to Cypress, just 15 miles away. I enrolled at Cypress College, where, on the first day of school while I was eating lunch, the assistant coach, Tom Lubin, noticed my height (now 6'9"), approached me, and asked, "Are you planning on playing basketball?" Tom's uncle was Frank Lubin, UCLA All-American and starting center for the 1936 U.S. Olympic team. I said, "No. I'd like to, but my stepfather won't let me." He said he would take care of that, and every day after my last class, he met me on the outside courts (we didn't have a gym because the school was only two years old), where he taught me the hook shot Frank had taught him. He also checked my vertical jump by asking me to jump with two feet and touch the rim as many times in succession as I could. I was not able to do it twice.

Tom introduced me to Don Johnson, head coach and an All-American basketball player at UCLA under John Wooden. Coach Johnson wanted me on the team, but I told him and Lubin, "There is no way. If my stepfather knew I was staying after school to play basketball, he would kill me."

Somehow, Tom was able to sweet-talk my stepfather into it. I made the team because I was 6'9", certainly not due to my basketball skills. I was well-coached, worked hard, and became a good player my sophomore year, so good that John Wooden asked me to come to UCLA and back up Bill Walton, a great player out of Helix High School, La Mesa, California (near San Diego).

While Bill was playing freshman basketball (freshmen were not allowed on varsity), I red-shirted, which means I practiced but didn't suit up. That saved me a year of eligibility. The next year, I was a junior while Walton became a sophomore. Words cannot explain how skilled this young man was at age 18. Because Bill had bad knees, which would stiffen if he was out of action for longer than a minute, I sat the bench for two years, coming in only at the end of games when the victories were ensured.

The 1972 Summer Olympics in Munich occurred between my junior and senior years. Walton was invited to try out, but mostly because of his knees, he felt he should not have to try out, but rather be given an automatic spot on the team. I fully agree with him. The crazy Olympic Committee (or Coach Hank Iba, maybe) didn't agree so Bill didn't go to the Air Force Academy in Colorado for the trials. Coach Wooden asked the committee if I could go as Bill's replacement. He told them, "Swen probably won't make the team; he just needs the experience." But Coach knew better. They agreed, and as it happened, I led the entire camp in scoring, and to the surprise of the world (not Coach Wooden), I made the team.

During training in Hawaii at the submarine base in Honolulu, I lost 25 pounds because of the stupidity of Hank Iba and his staff, John Bach and Don Haskins. We practiced three times a day, and our meals were always immediately following practice. I had no appetite after a hard workout because I filled my belly with liquids immediately after, due to profuse sweating as a result of practicing on an outside, covered court. And all of us know how humid it is in Hawaii. Consequently, my appetite for food did not surface until about 45 minutes later. The mess hall was closed at that time, so I was not ever able to eat a meal.

I asked Iba and his staff if they could provide me food later but they said, "No." One week later, after losing 25 pounds, I asked again and received the same reply. Weak and thin, I quit, and they gladly sent me home. It seemed John Bach was the one most pleased. But I had made my mark, and my name was on the lips of every NBA and ABA scout.

In those days, Pizza Hut sponsored the Pizza Hut Basketball Classic, a nationally televised all-star game in Las Vegas, where the best college seniors were invited to play. Of course, Walton was invited, but he wasn't interested. Coach Wooden approached Pizza Hut and asked if I could take Bill's place just so I could get the experience and the scouts could see me in action. Few had ever seen me play. They agreed.

I was a member of the West Team. We had one practice, the day before the game. In that practice, our starting center landed on his back and was hurt to the point that he was not able to play in the game. There was only one other center: me. I played the entire game and was MVP, with 34 points and 25 rebounds, largely due to Ed Ratleff (Long Beach State) passing me the basketball.

As a result, I was selected 16th in the first round of the NBA draft by the Milwaukee Bucks. I am, to date, the only player in the history of NCAA basketball to be drafted in the first round who did not start a college game. The Bucks' incumbent center was none other than Kareem Abdul-Jabbar. For two years, I had been sitting on the bench behind Walton, so I was not about to sit behind another UCLA center. I wanted to play and show people what I could do. It was my time. So, I signed with the Virginia Squires of the ABA. The plan worked beautifully as I was ABA Rookie of the Year, two-time ABA All-Star, and ABA leading rebounder.

When my third season ended, the ABA folded and four teams joined the NBA. Every ABA player was to become a free agent, but before that was official, I quickly signed with the Bucks, who had my NBA rights. Kareem had already been traded to the Lakers. In the NBA, I played for the Bucks, the Buffalo Braves, the San Diego Clippers, and the Lakers. During that time, I led the NBA in rebounds, had a 53.7 field goal percentage (45th all-time), and set some records, one of which is still standing: 18 defensive rebounds in one half of a game. I was also able to qualify as one of the few elite members of the NBA 30/30 Club, scoring 30 points and grabbing 33 rebounds in the same game.

In five short years, from Cypress College to the ABA, I went from an unknown college backup center to a professional starter and one of the best centers in the game. How does that happen? How does someone with virtually no game experience gain that much ground in such a short period of time? There is only one answer: hard work and crash-course coaching.

Crash-Course Coaching

When I joined the Cypress College team, it was very clear to Don Johnson and Tom Lubin that I needed a crash course in post play if I was going to become a contributing player. My disadvantage was that the clock was ticking, but I had two huge advantages: Don Johnson taught the fundamentals exactly like his college coach, John Wooden, and Tom Lubin, the nephew of the great Frank Lubin, was an expert in post play, particularly offensive post play.

My freshman year, I played behind a very experienced and skilled center who kicked my tail every day for most of the season. He scored at will against me, stole almost every rebound away from me, and blocked as many of my shots as he wanted to. As if that was not enough, Don Johnson gave me no slack or special treatment at all. He had high expectations for me and incessantly demanded I perform at the level the rest of the players were already at. It was a regular occurrence for him to jump all over my case about one thing or another (e.g., I was too high when pivoting, ran too slowly, made a cut too slowly, didn't get that rebound when I should have, didn't challenge a shot when I should have). Rarely did Johnson hand me a compliment. In short, I thought about quitting the team almost every day. But I didn't, you see; I loved basketball.

Tom Lubin continued, every day, to coach me on the post moves and post footwork. He cut me no slack either. When I did something wrong, he had me do it again and again and again. When I got discouraged, he reminded me of how much progress I had made. When I got a little cocky because I had made an improvement, he reminded me of how far I still had to go.

But there were others that complemented Johnson's and Lubin's crash course. Bruce Randall, an ex-Cypress student and volunteer assistant coach, who was 6'3" and weighed over 300 pounds, had me play one-on-one against him while he beat the crap out of me. Mark Miller, another teammate, did the same and had no mercy during scrimmages; he would hurt me when he drove to the basket to score and then encouraged me to stop him the next time. Russ Sharples, a Cypress 6'6" jumping jack, took me aside after a practice and taught me how to jump. He told me, "You jump like a girl" and taught me to bend my legs to 90 degrees and explode. Russ believed, as I believe now and always will: you don't need to lift weights to become a leaper. The key to vertical improvement is to jump as high as you can and, each day, get a little higher. Nothing will improve jumping like jumping.

In their one-season crash course on post play, Johnson and Lubin taught me the basics for how to get open, how to receive the basketball, how to maneuver around a defender to get to the offensive boards, and how to block out.

Against Orange Coast College, the second-to-last game of the season, Johnson called me off the bench. We were behind by 10 points. The first thing I did was use Sharples' method of jumping to block the jump shot of the opposing center. The next thing I remember was making a hook shot. The rest is rather muddy, but we won the game, and the stat sheet showed I had 15 points and 10 rebounds. The next game, I again came off the bench, this time to score 20 points and pull down 15 rebounds. The season had come to an end, but my love for the game had not. The crash course worked, but I needed one more thing—experience—and that meant hard work.

Hard Work

Tom Lubin knew I needed experience if I was going to be a dominant force in the middle for Cypress my sophomore year, and the best place to get experience was on the playgrounds of Los Angeles. Between the end of my freshman season and the beginning of school the next year, Lubin regularly drove me to L.A. and fed me to the wolves. What a great guy! Without exception, I was the only white guy in the gym every Saturday. It was painful at first. Nobody knew me and I had a difficult time talking them into letting me play. Our first trip, I stood on the sidelines for two hours. Then Tom and I went home.

Our second trip to the same gym, I talked somebody into letting me play on his team. The man I was playing was 6'7" and could jump out of the gym. The first time he had the ball at the low post, he backed me under the basket, jumped over me, and dunked the ball so hard, the other eight players—yes, even those on my team—fell on the floor laughing.

But I learned how to get on a team. Once on the floor, I also learned, very quickly, the skills I had were only skills at that point. They needed to go through a testing phase in order to work in actual competition. In other words, I had a hook shot that I could make nine out of 10 times with no one guarding me, but in L.A., they made it very difficult for me to get that off. I could catch the basketball well, but in L.A., I couldn't get open. I could jump above the rim, but those quick L.A. jumping jacks got to the rebound before me. Through trial, error, pain, and embarrassment, I figured all of it out, and in August, one month before my sophomore year, I was always picked first, they fed me the ball, and we won almost every game.

By the way, remember that guy that dunked on me? Three Saturdays later, we were matched up again. This time, I backed him up and dunked on him so hard the basket shook for 10 seconds, and he received the same embarrassing humiliation from the other players that I did.

Between Saturdays, I worked on my skills and strength back home. I pumped iron three days a week (mainly clean and jerk and military press) and put on 10 pounds of muscle. I religiously worked on my vertical jump by dunking the ball while wearing a 30-pound weight jacket, as well as grabbing the ball off the arm of the McCall's basketball rebounder. My brother and I played one-on-one at the low post where the defender was allowed to do whatever was necessary to keep the other player away from the basket. For hand and forearm strength, I used two tools. I found a ball-shaped rock that I could not pick up with one hand, took it home and put it next to my desk in the bedroom, and, while doing homework, tried picking it up over and over again. In time, I was able to lift it with no problem. The other tool I used was a hand gripper. I worked that contraption out so much—several times every evening—that I eventually snapped the spring.

That, my friends, leads me to the purpose of this book, which is to provide instruction for putting a post player through a crash course in post play. I was crash-coursed from beginner to advanced in one year, and there is no doubt in my mind that it is possible for a coach to do the same with a young post player. The contents of this book, when applied, will help enable a coach or parent to successfully put a post player through the crash course as well. However, by no means are the concepts presented here exclusively for beginners; they will take the more experienced player to the highest level of the game. If a college center, for example, learns my methods for getting open, sealing, drop-stepping, and the two-move set, it will help him be able to compete in the NBA or Europe.

As you might imagine, when conducting my "Play Post Like the Pros" clinics around the world, coaches have asked many questions. Additional questions have been asked via email or by phone. Everywhere I go, the same questions are asked. For the purpose of helping those who were not able to contact me, or those who have never thought about asking an expert, I have created this publication, which answers the questions that were presented most often.

Some of the chapters in this book contain the findings of my off-season lab work. Those chapters cover: how to get a post player to dominate the boards, how to get a post player to become a defensive force around the basket, the moves a post player should have, and how to seal at the low post. One chapter deals with something I learned before playing basketball: how to teach a player to catch the ball. And two chapters present what I learned after retiring from the NBA: the incredible value of the drop step as a primary weapon, and the fundamentals of post play and how to teach them.

Before you follow me to the first chapter, let me warn you: some of my methods may be different and unconventional compared to what you may have learned and are using now. But I assure you, they are better because they work at the highest level of basketball.

Lastly, do you want to win more games? Make the effort to develop the post player and use that player. There are no more excuses; you now have the book. Best wishes.

To access free online video demonstrating the basics of sound post play, scan the following QR code with a smartphone or go to coacheschoice.com/Developing-a-great-basketball-post-player-Video.

coacheschoice.com/Developing-a-great-basketball-post-player-Video

CHAPTER 1

What Value Is a Post Player to My Team?

I have a big kid, but it's going to take a lot of work. To be honest, I don't really think we need him. We run a five-man perimeter motion offense, and it's working for us. We aren't very tall, but we're quick. We leave the post area open so we can drive to the basket and make basket and backdoor cuts, and the open space allows us to drive, which we're good at.

History Shows the Importance of Getting the Ball to the Post

The real question here is not "What value is the post player?" but rather: "What value to the offense is the post position?" In other words, coaches do not know if the many hours invested in training the raw post player will pay off with increased point production per possession.

At UCLA, we ran the high-post offense or a variation thereof. However, some may not know, Coach Wooden ran that system his entire career, while coaching high school teams in Kentucky and Indiana, an NAIA team at Indiana State, and an NCAA team at UCLA.

To Coach Wooden, using the post for offensive production was non-negotiable. In this offense, the post was always used, every play, to open things up for the other players. For example, during the 1964 and 1965 seasons (his first two championship teams), when the ball went to Fred Slaughter at the high post, Gail Goodrich and Walt Hazzard, our main scorers, would start making their cuts to get open down the middle and on the sides. Any time the ball went to the post, screening took place to get those two players open. At times, Hazzard would simply cut to the basket and post up. As a very tall and strong guard in his day, he was very dangerous down there. When Fred had the ball at the high post, he could pass to anyone who was open. So, if any defender helped to stop Goodrich and Hazzard, an immediate opening was there, and Fred would always find them. Also, he could score from up there, and that made it even more difficult for the defense.

There is a misconception that Coach Wooden ran the same offense every year. Nothing could be further from the truth. Almost every season, Coach adjusted the offense to meet the needs of the players. The post was always used and the offensive principles were always the same, but the movements and plays were changed, depending on the personnel that particular season. Some think he completely changed the offense when he acquired Kareem Abdul-Jabbar, then known as Lewis Alcindor. In reality, that change may have been the smallest one he made in all his years. It was still the high-post offense, but with one forward becoming the low post, and the other forward coming to the high post. Every year Wooden coached, he used the post. In fact, getting the ball there was the priority.

When I played at UCLA, the center was Bill Walton. Bill had freedom to go to the low or high post. That team exemplified, more than any other UCLA team, how valuable the post player is when he is able to get open anywhere in the post area to receive the ball. When Bill had the ball, either he was going to score or somebody was going to have a high-percentage shot. He was an amazing passer with a high degree of team spirit and a skilled scorer—the trifecta of any great offensive player.

But Wooden was not the only coach to use the post. In that day, every coach did. It was understood, other than in the fast break, the high-percentage shot must go through the post because the ball at the post was an immediate scoring threat.

No one knew this better than Pete Francis Newell, who, when coaching the University of California at Berkeley, faced the University of San Francisco with the great Bill Russell. If it were not for their good shooting center, Darrall Imhoff, fouling out in the second half, UC Berkeley could very well have won the game against the number-one ranked team that went on to win the national championship that year.

In that game, all Newell did for his offensive strategy was place Imhoff at the high post. On one wing, he ran a screen for a skilled offensive guard/forward who was great driving to the basket. No USF player was capable of stopping him except Russell (guarding Imhoff), who would drop down to the basket to block the shot. However, whenever Berkeley saw Russell leave Imhoff, they would pass the ball to him and Imhoff rarely missed from that area. At halftime, Berkeley was ahead in the score and in control of the game. So there we have another good reason to get the ball to the post: to keep a good shot blocker busy.

Has Anything Changed?

Offensively, the post (high or low) is not used to that extent today, particularly at the high school level. With fewer post players being developed at the prep level, fewer skilled post players enter college. Hence, today, we see, as a percentage, a dearth of true post players in college and in the NBA.

With that said, you may be asking, "So what's the big deal with post play? The game has changed. We don't need a true post anymore." As a kid in Holland, I played soccer. I believe it helped me with basketball because the two sports are alike in that there is a goal and a team is trying to score. But here is another commonality: from soccer team to soccer team, the offensive styles vary, but there is always one constant; to score, the ball must get to the middle within striking distance from the goal.

In soccer, there is definitely a point guard who is in the middle, a distance from the goal. There are wings just like in basketball. And there is a post player very close to the goal, just like in basketball. As play goes on, from time to time, one player will sprint into the middle, somewhere between the point and the player by the goal. That is soccer's high post. Once the ball gets there, the defense collapses in an attempt to block the direct kick. When the ball is passed to the wing from there, that player is open. He may attempt a score, pass back to the high post, or opt to kick back to the point. In other words, getting the ball into the middle of the field, within striking distance of the goal, distorts the defense and opens up opportunities.

If you ask a soccer coach to leave that high-post area open and to not put a player there, he will tell you you're crazy (in German, Italian, Spanish, or whatever language he speaks). I say, if you don't use the post in basketball, well, you are crazy. The immediate threat of the score from the middle is pivotal to developing a high-percentage shot. It is true in soccer, and it's true in basketball. Take the ball out of the middle, and everything becomes more difficult. Get the ball to the post, and things begin to look bright.

The Motion Offense

Coaches who use a motion-style offense and do not get the ball into the post area have been deceived. They believe the backdoor cut, screen and roll, and the cut down the middle can replace the ball in the hands of the post player. The backdoor pass from guard to forward is not nearly as effective as from high post to forward because it is a long pass that takes more time, and most of the time, the forward receives the ball while still six to eight feet from the rim. In the post-to-forward backdoor play, it's a quick pass/ pass/score situation. The roll in the ball screen is a good move and should be used, but it does not collapse the defense. The basket cut, like the UCLA cut, will drop, at most, one defensive player to help, and that player will be the weakside defender. His man is completely on the other side of the half-court and is not an immediate scoring threat. When the ball is at the high post, for example, all five players are scoring threats.

When I coached, this is exactly what I did. I used the post, even if I didn't have a tall post player, and it worked beautifully. Granted, the ideal situation is to have a Bill Walton operating at the low and high post; that's why you've got to give that tall player a chance. But the post player can actually be almost any height if he can score and pass from there. Once I had a 5'10" high-post player, and he was a problem for the other team.

But there's nothing like having a Walton with the ball down low or high. When he had the basketball, screeners and cutters were rapidly moving on both sides of the half-court. Bill was a prolific scorer from the low post, and there has never been a better passing center from the high post, or from anywhere. He always found the open man. Bill was not a good 15-foot shooter, so the only reason he came up high was for pressure release. For that reason, Coach filled the high post most of the time with the great Jamaal Wilkes, or Keith Wilkes as he was called then.

But the mere fact that the ball was passed into Bill's hands around the post area dropped the defense down immediately, particularly when it looked like he was going to try to score. And those of us who played with Bill at UCLA or with the Portland Trail Blazers know: when Walton had the ball, the possibility of an uncontested lay-up or jump shot was high. Something good was going to go down.

The Low Post

Before leaving this chapter, I want you to know, while getting the ball to the high post is very important to creating a high-percentage shot, getting it to the low post is also effective. The very fact that the ball is close to the basket in the middle area—low, mid, or high—poses an immediate scoring threat for the defense and distorts it as defenders leave their assignments to plug up the middle. With the ball in Kareem's hands at the low post and with his ability to pass, the outside shot opened up as players either moved to an opening, cut down the middle, or employed a screening situation on the weakside.

Do you have a tall player who needs work to become a contributor? Let me tell you a quick story and with this I conclude. As a high school junior, I was the second-tallest boy in the school at 6'4". I tried out for the basketball team and was cut. The rest is history.

Now go find that tall drink of water and get going.

Key Points

- Using the post is essential for effective offense.
- The post is a key component in other team sports where goals are scored.
- Getting the ball to the low post is as effective as to the high post.

CHAPTER 2

How Can I Improve My Post Player's Ability to Catch the Ball?

Good Hands and Bad Hands

Some people simply cannot catch a ball. When the ball approaches them, they stick out their hands and turn their head sideways, like they are about to make contact with something poisonous or explosive. This is because they have had bad painful experiences when catching, like the ball hitting them square on the nose or mouth. But those people are usually very young. Once we have experience at catching, we learn to avoid those painful situations one way or the other. We learn to catch the ball.

Yet, some teenage basketball players still have trouble consistently securing the ball without some degree of fumbling. We label these young people as "receiving disabled" and give up hope. We believe that if they haven't learned to catch properly by age 12 or so, they have a handicap that perhaps can be improved slightly, but can never be brought to normality.

In the classroom, teachers are quick to label children as learning disabled in the area of reading. While others grasp the sound to letter correspondence and learn to decode without too much trouble, others are not so quick to do so. For example, the fact that the letters "ei" can represent the sounds "I" like in the word "either," "E" like in "receive," and "A" (like in "veil") is confusing. Add the fact that, when "gh" is added to the end of "ei," that four-letter grapheme can also represent the sound "A" (like in "weight") as well as "I" (like in "height"), and you have even more complexity and difficulty. But are children who are slow to grasp this level of decoding disabled? The word *disabled* connotes such doomsday finality and depressive hopelessness. Are they really disabled, or do they just need more time and perhaps some additional instruction to be able to be fluent readers with good comprehension?

I was born in The Netherlands and came to the U.S. when I was nine years old. One week after my arrival, I entered fourth grade. My knowledge of English was "Yes," "No," and counting to 10. That's what I learned of English in third grade back in Holland. Although I had a great fourth-grade teacher, learning to read English was difficult, and I was behind the class for the entire year and probably all through elementary school. But one middle school summer, I read the entire series of The Hardy Boys, and I more than caught up. Was I learning disabled? No. I just needed a lot of practice learning the English written code. It took time for me to recognize words and learn how to decode new words.

So you have a somewhat-grown-up post player who has trouble catching a ball and you have tried everything. Rest easy; most people can learn to catch a ball rather well, but, like learning to read, it comes naturally for some, and those who have more trouble just need some pointers and a lot more guided practice.

Definition of a Catch

The definition of a catch is: when the player immediately gets the basketball in his hands, ready to do something with it. A proper catch is when the ball is grabbed and *secured* by both hands. It does not have to be simultaneous, but it should be close.

Learning by Doing

My first love was baseball, although I never played on a team. When we were teenagers, my brother Ibo and I would often sneak off to Spud Field, a baseball field in Long Beach, California's Signal Hill area. We played "High and Far." With mitts and ball, Ibo stood in center field, and I stood in right. Ibo threw the ball to me, but as high as he could. The higher the better because his wish (the varmint) was to make me drop the ball. The first one to drop three balls lost.

No excuses were permitted. For example, if my "little" brother threw it off to the side, too long, or way too short, and I couldn't get it, he won and I lost. Of course, there was an understanding; the point was to make the other miss by throwing the baseball very high, but occasionally, my brother would toss one that was out of the way so that I would have to dart after it and catch it on the run. Looking back, I think he often did this, trying to defeat his big brother. (He was always trying to beat me at everything.) My memory is not completely clear, but I would not rule out the possibility that I may have thrown him a challenging one once or twice also, particularly if I was behind in a game. Hey! You can't let your little brother beat you; he would have difficulty getting his inflated head in the front door when we got home, and, once inside, he would be impossible to live with!

The point of the story is: for learning how to catch a ball properly and consistently, there is no substitute for repetition, and if you can put some competition in the mix, it's even more effective practice. Regarding repetition and practice, Grantland Rice, the sportswriter of the Great Depression, wrote the following poem:

How to Be a Champion

You wonder how they do it,
You look to see the knack,
You watch the foot in action,
Or the shoulder or the back.

But when you spot the answer
Where the higher glamours lurk,
You'll find in moving higher
Up the laurel-covered spire,
That most of it is practice,
And the rest of it is work.

Through playing High and Far, Ibo and I learned how to catch a fly ball. We didn't have anyone to tell us how to scout the ball's path or hold a mitt. We learned through trial and error, and that learning was accelerated by the fear of losing the game.

High and Far was not the only catching game Ibo and I played. Another one was a behind-the-back passing competition. Standing four feet apart, I threw him the ball from behind my back with the right hand. I threw it to his right hand. Ibo caught the ball with his right hand (no left hand involved) and, with no hesitation, threw me a behind-the-back pass to my right hand. We played until one of us dropped the ball or threw an uncatchable pass.

For this game and for High and Far, we didn't always compete against each other; often, we would set a goal for consecutive catches and try to reach it. For the behind-the-back game, we once reached 200. I think he was the one who dropped the ball. Of course, we also did this game with the left hand.

It almost doesn't matter what games you play; it's catching the ball a thousand times that does the trick. Through repetition, players learn what works and what doesn't work. Teachers call this process "learning by doing." Coaches should devise uncomplicated drills that provide lots of practice catching. At first, of course, especially for the player who needs a lot of work, the drills would consist of simply catching a ball thrown normally, directly at the player. But as improvement is realized, difficulty is increased, and receiving is more challenging. Following are three more advanced drills that work well:

- *Bad pass drill:* The pass is thrown out of the player's reach. This will get him to move his feet and get his feet under the ball instead of reaching. Reaching, rather than moving the feet to the point where the ball will land, is a major reason for fumbles.
- *Scissor distraction drill:* The coach passes the ball to the post player while another player moves their arms, in scissor motion, in the path of the ball. That player cannot touch the ball, however.

- *Wrestle drill:* The coach is the passer. The offensive post player is in a low-post position with the defender directly behind. On a signal, the defense wrestles the offense to get the pass. The coach varies when the ball is passed. He can let the players wrestle a bit first or pass it quickly. He can also throw bad passes, almost directly to the defensive player, alternate offense to defense, and keep score.

Guided Practice Using Key Points

In my opinion, these drills, and additional activities the coach comes up with, should first be done with absolutely no instruction. Some players' skills will improve greatly using this method exclusively, because they are able to figure things out on their own, without a coach's instructions. But if the coach notices mechanical issues, the coach should begin to provide guided practice through teaching key points. While the player is catching, the coach provides the necessary verbal instructions, based on fundamental errors the player is making, to help the player be more successful. The act of giving only the necessary information is called "guided practice." The information provided is called a "key point." A key point is a fundamental detail (e.g., the follow-through for the jump shot) that, if not done correctly, hinders success.

Most coaches have never taken the time to write down the key points for receiving the basketball. Some may have books by great basketball coaches that provide lists of important considerations, but they have never analyzed catching themselves. Coach Wooden took an entire summer to master this one subject and wrote all of it down in *Practical Modern Basketball*. You can take the shortcut and buy a copy, but there's a better way. Go out in the gym with a pen and paper, pass the ball with other coaches, and write down the key points as you discover them. When you teach, you'll probably come up with another key or two and it's very possible you will eliminate one or two you initially wrote down. Remember, a "key point" is something that, if not done correctly, will cause failure. And what is a key point for one coach may not be for another. If you believe it to be true, it's true.

You cannot know what the player's problems are unless you know what the keys are. His problem will always be related to one or more of the key points. If not, you've missed a key. Get it?

While playing High and Far with Ibo, I taught myself five things (key points) that helped me. I learned all of them the hard way, but I learned them.

- *To get my glove under the ball.* The goal was to get the angle of the glove perpendicular to the flight of the ball so the ball had a good view of the pocket. This was easy when catching underhanded, but more difficult for the overhand catch (with the glove in a position as if I were going to give someone a high five).

In the overhand catch, the farther my glove was in front of me, the more the glove angle dropped (top of the glove moving forward), leaving the pocket invisible to the ball. When catching the baseball this way, I learned to catch it almost directly over my head (as opposed to in front of me), but just a little in front.

- *To keep my eye on the ball, all the way to the glove.* When I took my eyes off the ball, it often hit the side, the butt, or the end of the glove. Keeping my eyes on the ball increased the chances of the ball coming directly to the glove pocket.
- *To soften the catch.* I sometimes dropped the ball because it hit my glove and bounced out. I learned to eliminate that bounce (or bump) by making contact with the ball with arms extended and, as soon as the ball made contact with my glove, to lessen the impact by bringing the ball to me.
- *To secure the ball in the glove with the free hand.* This occurs at the same time as softening the catch. As soon as the ball touched my glove, I trapped it with the other hand. This is sometimes referred to as the block-and-tuck method of catching and is particularly important when catching the ball in the overhand position, as the ball can quickly drop out of the glove to the ground.
- *To bring the ball (in the glove and tucked with the free hand) to the chest for extra protection.* This point was particularly important when I was making a diving catch, which I often had to do when catching my brother's throws.

Four Key Points for Receiving

I'd like to say, when I began basketball, I fumbled the ball when it was passed to me in the post, but I actually had developed very good hands through playing High and Far and just doing a lot of catching with my brother; through trial and error, I was able to catch a ball successfully no matter how bad the pass was. In other words, I had mastered the Key Points for Catching:

- *Meet the ball.* Many passes are stolen or fumbled because the defender has a hand close by. The most important thing is for the player to get that ball, even if he loses a little real estate.
- *See the ball to the hands.* When the ball makes contact with the hand, the eyes should see it and then quickly move away.
- *Soften the catch/block and tuck.* The player should reach for the ball and bring it softly to him, trying to eliminate any sound when the ball contacts the hands. The block-and-tuck method of receiving is not a one-handed catch as some think. It is not the traditional two-handed catch either, where both hands touch the ball at the same time. The position of the hands for the traditional two-handed catch leaves too much space between the hands, enough for a ball to slip through. Young players often fumble using this method. Block and tuck ensures the ball is stopped with one hand, and then quickly secured with the other.

Figure 2- 1. The block-and-tuck method
for catching the basketball

- *Secure the ball.* The player doesn't have to bring the ball all the way to the chest, or below the chin as some promote; at times, that might bring the ball too close to the defensive player. Exactly how far away from the body or how high the ball should be depends on where the defense (both the on-ball defender and his teammates who may be coming to steal the ball) is located. The reality is: the post player will probably move the ball around a bit to keep it safe. But the ball must be secured to a degree where it cannot be slapped away. This will require elbows to be out a bit and the ball to be fairly close to the body.

  My brother Ibo and I played a little ballistic game called a Tomahawk Drill often, and it greatly helped my strength when holding the basketball. It's very simple. Facing each other and about arm's distance apart, we each held a basketball. While I held my basketball tightly, Ibo raised his basketball high in the air and then tomahawked it down on my basketball, trying to dislodge it from my hands. Immediately, I did the same. We continued alternating smashes until one of us lost the ball.

How to Teach

The best way to teach these four basics is to do the following:

- Throw a lot of passes to a player, beginning with easy ones and then making it more difficult so there are fumbles. When you see a fumble, throw the same pass again. Then mix it up, throwing other passes and coming back to the difficult one.

Don't teach the player anything at this point; they must figure stuff out on their own first, as much as they can. While this is going on, take mental notes of which of the four key points the player needs help with. Two players can also do this drill while the coach observes.

- Then, teach the second step (see the ball to the hands) and combine with the first step (meet the ball). Then teach the third step (soften the catch/block and tuck) and combine with the first and second steps. And so on. Remember to demonstrate and provide the rationale for each step.

These drills are good, but their main benefit is that they provide lots of catching practice in a somewhat competitive environment; the player does not want to miss a pass. As Coach Wooden said, "Repetition is the key to learning."

So, when you teach your post player to improve his hands, first do a thorough job of demonstrating and explaining the details. Only after the player completely understands the operation of the skill can you move to having him try it. While he is imitating what he saw you do, correct everything but don't stop him if you can help it; he needs repetition. The player will learn by doing. But there's one more thing your post player must know which will result in the development of better hands: responsibility.

Responsibility

The coach must make it very clear to the post player that, no matter how bad a pass may be, he is responsible for securing the basketball. This goes back to the High and Far game Ibo and I played; if one of us failed to catch the ball, no degree of blame could be placed on the passer, no matter how bad the pass was. When a coach allows fault to be applied to the passer in certain situations, the receiver will most certainly not work as hard for those balls that are difficult to get to. By the way, this concept is also true for the screen. As Coach Wooden made perfectly clear, the sole responsibility for getting open when using a screen belongs exclusively to the cutter, not the screener. With this rule understood and enforced, the cutters will work much harder to get open, and the screeners will be less likely to get called for a moving screen.

Key Points

- Almost everyone can learn to catch well.
- The coach must take responsibility for the problem and for teaching.
- Players must learn by doing.
- Coaches must provide guided practice.

CHAPTER 3

Why Won't They Pass the Ball Into the Post?

How many times have I sat watching a high school basketball game and seen the following scenario? The post player has his defender behind him; the perimeter player has the ball, ready to pass; he looks into the post for a half second with not an ounce of interest, then passes the ball to another player. I've seen the cold-shoulder treatment more times than I've had to duck going through 6'8" doorways. I can still hear the parents (of the post player, of course) yelling, "Pass the ball in! Pass the ball to the post! He is open!"

What's the reason? Why don't those guards and forwards pass to those wonderful people down low? The kid is tall and has a height advantage. He's a nice kid. So why isn't that ball going in there? Why do they look at him on the wing with the ball over their heads, acting like they're ready to launch a pass toward the post, and then, almost as if they're alternatively programmed, change course with apparently no reason? And there the post player stands, bewildered, hands still in the air, waiting for the pass, with a facial expression that communicates, "I don't get it; I was open." Is there a natural dislike between the outside and the inside? Is there a secret Perimeter Club, the DGBP (Don't Give the Ball to the Post), where players take a pledge to never pass it in?

> *"I, a member of the DGBP Club, promise to never, no matter what— be it pressure by the coach, the post player, or his parents—pass the basketball to a post player. I understand, if I fail to abide by this pledge and, in a moment of weakness, give a post player the basketball, I will immediately be excommunicated from the club."*

Ridiculous, right? So if there is no perimeter agenda, what does the post player have to do to get the ball? Does he have to take the guards and forwards to dinner? Perhaps his parents should, with an ulterior motive and hope for a return on their investment, host a team party, reluctantly feed those selfish little undersized brats, and announce, after dinner, "Did you enjoy the meal? See my kid here? He's a nice boy. Next time you see him open in the post, please give him the ball."

The Other Perspective

Those who wonder why the post player is being slighted will find the answers when they look at things from the perimeter perspective. It's easy to draw conclusions when viewing things from one side, and oftentimes those conclusions are wrong. From the perspective of the post (and that includes the parents), they are open to receive the ball. However, let's walk just 15 feet from the block to the three-point line, turn around to look at the post area, and see what things look like from that vantage point. We will see it's quite different, in fact, completely different.

What the post player sees is his teammate with the ball, looking into the post. As a post player, with the defender pretty much behind me, I do not see him posing any threat to a completed pass. I know, if he does try to get around me, I'll just get in his path and go get the ball. But my perimeter passer does not see the same picture. He sees, if he does pass the ball in, the pass is directed not only at me, but also at the defender. In other words, he sees a somewhat risky passing situation. So we have, on the one hand, me, thinking the odds of me catching the pass are extremely good, in fact perfect, and, on the other hand, my teammate not nearly so certain.

I have interviewed many guards and forwards and asked them why they don't pass the ball into the post. I have boiled their responses down to three reasons:

- "Based on experience, I didn't think he could catch the ball safely. I thought if I threw it in, the ball would be knocked away. And guess whose fault that is going to be? Mine. And I'll be sitting on the bench before you can say, 'Turnover.'"
- "Why should I throw it in? He can't score."
- "If I throw the ball in, he's not going to throw it back out. If I'm expected to give the ball to the post, the post should be expected to throw it back out when he doesn't have a good situation or sees a better one on the perimeter."

Who Can Fix This Problem?

In order to resolve any issue between two people, each of the parties must assume full responsibility and blame and do what needs to be done to solve it from their end. Suppose a post player's father (bless his heart) should say after a game, "Son, there were two times when you were wide open in the post and neither Johnny nor Beauford passed you the ball." The post player's instant response should be, "Dad, I know I was wide open, and I must be doing something wrong for them not to pass it in." That's taking full responsibility.

> *In order to begin resolving any issue between two parties,*
> *each must assume full responsibility and blame.*

The second step for solving a disagreement is to see the issue from the other perspective. In this case, the perimeter players are not passing the ball into the post when they could, for one (or more) of three reasons: Risk of a turnover, not a high-percentage play, or the black hole. Hey! I don't blame them. So, the post player must change. He must become a safe target, a scorer, and a distributor. If that doesn't solve the problem, we'll have to give the perimeter players an IQ test.

My first year playing basketball, as a freshman at Cypress College, I sat the bench except for the last three games of the season. That's when I finally began to show I could play this game a little. In those last three games, I averaged 18 points, but got most of them off the offensive boards; they wouldn't pass the ball in to me because I was new and they didn't know if I could catch the ball or what I could do with it should I get it.

That summer, I lifted weights religiously, gaining 15 pounds of muscle, and my younger brother and I played one-on-one. Our favorite game was a ballistic, war-like, one-on-one basketball wrestling match. There were only two rules: "No points if you don't dunk the basketball" and "No punching." When I had the ball, I backed into him until he hit me with a forearm or slammed his body into mine. His goal was to keep me away from the rim, and whatever he needed to do, short of punching me, was legal. As he continued to push and slam me, I increased the pressure until I felt he was pushing so hard, his balance was too far forward. That's when I spun around him to get to the basket. Most of the time, he anticipated it and bulldozed me out-of-bounds. Then I would come back in and do the same thing until I got the dunk, and oftentimes he was pushing me even as I elevated. Then it was his turn.

This drill not only got me stronger and in great shape, it also taught me to release pressure by spinning around the defender. The more he pushed, the closer I got to the rim. It also developed me into a player who was looking for the high-percentage shot first (the one close in) before countering with a hook or jump shot.

To put all that work into game practice, I played all the pick-up basketball I could during the week in Orange County, and on weekends, I frequented the Los Angeles inner-city gymnasiums where, if you couldn't score inside, nobody was going to be crazy enough to pass you the ball. After all, if you lost a pick-up game, you were sitting out for a half hour or more. It was all about winning. I became very good at scoring that summer and my teammates had no reservation about passing me the ball.

As a result, the next season I was a greatly improved offensive post player. I averaged 26.4 points and 16.4 rebounds per game. And guess what? My teammates wanted to pass me the ball because they knew I could catch it, they were confident I would pass it back if I was double-covered (actually, I rarely passed the ball back out), and they knew I could score down there and help us win. And if there was anything my teammates loved, it was winning. Winning is cool.

In other words, in the off-season, I didn't naively think, *Next year, the coach will make sure they pass the ball to me.* Instead, I thought, *I'm going to get so good down there, they will know they are fools if they don't take advantage of me.*

Safely receiving the basketball was another area I improved in that summer, and it all happened during the pick-up games in Orange County and Los Angeles. When I became known as a scorer, my defender did everything he could to keep me from getting my hands on the basketball. In one game, he was very good at it, and after getting the ball stolen or deflected two times, my teammates stopped passing to me. That didn't feel very good. So I worked on it and regained their confidence. See Chapter 4 for details on how to teach your post player to get open.

So what about not being a black hole? How important is that? It is a very distant third in my opinion. When that ball goes into the post to a good scorer, it should not come back out unless absolutely necessary. I believe I can count on two hands the times I gave up and kicked the ball to a guard or forward on the perimeter.

So, the answer to the question, "Why don't my guards throw the ball in to my post player when he is open?" is: They don't think the post player can catch it safely, they don't believe it's a high-percentage play for the team, and they believe the ball won't come back out, with the first two being most prevalent in their minds.

Key Points

- The post player needs to understand that the perimeter player is not confident his pass will reach the post.
- The post player should take full responsibility for a completed pass.
- The post player should become a scorer.
- The post player should learn to get open.
- The post player should be a distributor (least important).

CHAPTER 4

How Do I Teach My Post Player to Get Open?

Chapter 3 (Why Won't They Pass the Ball Into the Post?) tackles the issue of perimeter players not passing the basketball into the post when it seems, both to the post player and especially the player's parents, that it is safe and wise to do so. What can be done? Shall we have a talk with the perimeter players? Shall we make them give up the ball? Shall we provide some incentives, such as candy, McDonald's gift certificates, or a little card that states the perimeter player is exempt from one suicide sprinting drill? No. The only logical solution, and the only one that will work for the long run, is for the post player to take full responsibility for developing himself into a scoring threat.

My survey results, when interviewing perimeter players, revealed three reasons why they don't pass the ball in: They are not confident the post player is as open as he thinks he is, they don't think he can score should he get the ball, and they think that if the ball does go in, it probably will not come back out. This chapter will address the first reason: They don't throw the ball in because they are not completely confident the player will seal off his defender and actually catch the ball.

What is going on in the perimeter player's mind? While the post player feels confident that the pass should be delivered and will surely be received, the perimeter player feels the chances of a completed pass are not nearly as high. If we were to ask the post player, "Were you open?" he would say, "Yes." If we were to ask the perimeter player, "Was the post open?" he would say, "No. I felt the defense had too much of a chance to cause a turnover."

Now we are getting at the issue. Who is right? In retail, the customer is always right because the customer is the one who makes the decision to buy or not to buy. The retailer must deliver what the customer wants or no purchase will be made. In basketball, the passer is always right for the same reason; he either buys or does not buy that the player is open. It's up to the post player to provide what the passer wants. The passer wants the post to be open, not open in the eyes of the post, but open in the eyes of the passer. Therefore, it is necessary to define what "open" means from the perimeter perspective.

In my professional career, I received the ball in the post thousands of times. Nobody was afraid to pass the ball to me because they knew I was going to receive it.

I can't remember one incident when I did not safely receive the basketball. I may have had to move out of ideal position, but I got the ball. As a result, my teammates had no hesitation about throwing the ball in.

It took time to convince them I was not going to let my defender intercept their passes, and it required an effort on my part to develop skill in getting open. Following, then, are the basics.

Use the Reverse

For getting open in the post, Bill Walton is the best I've seen; he was skilled at all of the steps and key points I am presenting. But there was something he habitually and deliberately did that moved the defense behind him: he was very good at reversing to the basket for the pass and did it often. When he was battling and wrestling for low-post position and he sensed the defender was moving away from behind him enough to create a lane for him to go to the basket, Bill quickly reversed to the hoop and often received the pass for the easy score. If you would like video, see the Memphis State vs. UCLA NCAA championship game from 1973. It was ridiculous how many times this happened. But once the defense got wise to that (I'm not going to name names, but it took him a long time), one fake of the reverse, and the defense moved back to protect the hoop and Bill received the ball at the low post with ease. If a player doesn't have the reverse, they are a one-dimensional player and easy to guard.

The Sideways Stance

High school post players are often taught, when they are positioned at the low post and the defender is behind them, to make contact with their backside to keep him there. This may work against a defender with a low intellect, but it will never keep competitive defenders between the post and the passer. The reason has to do with vision and space. Contact with the backside means the player cannot see the defender, unless they have eyes back there.

When the defender makes a move to get around the player, he will come into peripheral vision when it's too late to react. If the player has a little space between the two of them to work with (which he doesn't, but assume he does), he might be able to step in front of the defender. So, to add insult to injury, because there is no space between the two of them, no matter how quickly the player reacts by trying to block the defender away, the most he can do is allow the defender to get on his side, which is a huge red flag for the perimeter player who wants to pass the ball in.

The solution is what I call the sideways stance. When the post player commences to post up, say on the left side of the key (left side as seen from the top of the key), he positions himself on the line between his defender and the man with the ball. We will call this the "ball-defender line." His left forearm is in contact with the defender's chest (gently, not pushing) and the line through his shoulders is somewhat parallel to the ball-defender line. I say "parallel" because he steps below that line a bit in order to see both the ball and the defender.

Because he has vision and space, this position will enable him to keep himself between the passer and the defender no matter what his opponent does to get around. If the defender tries to get around over the top, the post player blocks his progress by stepping into his path with the left foot.

Figure 4-1. Sideways stance

Figure 4-2. Post player stepping with left foot to block player trying to get over the top

If the man attempts to go under to get around, the post player pivots on the left foot and drops the right foot back to block him out.

Figure 4-3. Post player stepping with right foot, toward baseline, to block defender trying to get around the bottom side

To develop this skill, it will take plenty of practice, working on the footwork without the defense first and then against another player. And mind you, because there is so much space for the defender to work in, it's impossible to keep a determined defender from getting around. But by the time he does, the perimeter player will probably already have passed the ball to the point, or to the high-post player if the post has sealed his man.

One last point on this: when he is positioned at the low post outside the lane, the player should never, never, never post up with his backside against the defender. He won't get open against a good one, and the passers will not be confident he is open. The passer will be much more assured the pass will be completed when the post player has created space between him and the defender and keeps the defender behind him.

Present a Juicy Target

When the post player positions himself on the ball-defender line, the perimeter player gains confidence the pass will be caught. But when he presents a juicy target, the passer gets even more assured. That is because an outstretched hand toward the ball, almost as if the post player is trying to grab it out of the passer's hands, communicates: "I want that basketball, I will catch it, and I can do something with it."

The one player in all of basketball history who provided the juiciest target was Bill Walton. Everyone, including the fans, knew that when Bill had the ball down low, something great was about to happen. He could score, and if he was double-teamed, he would pass the ball to an open teammate. No one was better at both. When Walton asked for the ball with his sign language, his hand was up above his head and pointed directly at the perimeter player with the basketball. His elbow was locked so his arm was completely straight, allowing his hand to get as close to the ball as possible. And here's something more important: his fingers were stretched to the full, his hand opened completely so the passer could see as large a target as possible. And with Bill's large meat hooks, that was quite a target.

Figure 4-4. Bill Walton posting up, providing a great target

You might ask, "But isn't a two-handed target better than a one-handed target?" The short answer is: "No." When the post player has both hands up, it means he has his back to the defender, which we have already established is not ideal positioning because it gives the defender an advantage. However, there are times when it is the right target, one of which is when the player flashes into the key to receive the pass. In that case, the sideways stance makes no sense; the player must catch the ball with both hands and make the immediate move to score.

Communication is a key component of basketball success. When we teach communication in basketball, it is almost exclusively on the defensive end of the floor. We instruct players to call out screens, say "Switch" when a player is screened well, and verbally identify matchups when transitioning from offense to defense. Where is the rule that states we are not to talk when on offense? Great football teams talk as much on the offensive side of the ball as on the defensive side.

When the post player is on the ball-defender line, and he is presenting a juicy target, he can increase the chances of that perimeter player throwing the pass by telling him he wants that round object down low. I had no hesitation doing so; when my teammate had the ball on the wing, and I sensed one ounce of doubt in his mind, I yelled, "Ball!" or "Give me the ball" or "Yes! Now!" Hey! Sometimes you just have to help your teammate make the right decision.

Other Ways to Get Open

So far, we have covered getting open when the post player is positioned on one side of the basket and the ball is passed to the wing on that same side. Other scenarios need to be covered, and they are all similar. Those situations are: moving across the lane to the ballside, down screening, and cutting down the lane. In each of these instances, the post player, not being on the ball-defender line, will get that position via one powerful and aggressive move: the spin move.

Moving Across the Lane

We will use the move going left to right from the point guard's view. In order to spin off the defender and in the direction of the basketball (on the right wing), the post player must maneuver himself to obtain a position about equal distance from the wing. The best way to do this is to make a convincing fake toward the baseline, moving the defender down a bit. Once this is accomplished, the player's right foot is planted close to the defender's right foot.

Immediately, he turns his shoulders counterclockwise with his upper body in a vertical position. (He will be using his upper back to get position.) As the shoulders turn, the upper back makes contact with the defender (smothering him, in a sense), and the post player literally rolls across the defender's upper body and in between him and the wing.

The torque of the shoulder rotation will turn the legs and feet; they have no choice. The post player then maintains contact and moves to the ball when it is passed.

Figure 4-5. Post player faking baseline with the right foot planted by the defender's right foot

Figure 4-6. Player's shoulders turned with upper back against defender

Down Screen

With the basketball at the guard position and the post player setting the down screen on the left side, the post player makes the identical move he made when going across the key; he plants his right foot by the defender's right foot and spins into the key. Note that the spin is not a stationary move. Like a ballet dancer making spin moves across the stage, the post player also moves. In this case, he spins into the middle of the key to receive the basketball.

Although this down screen spin move works best when the player slips the screen (i.e., makes his move before screening his teammate's defender) because it catches his defender off guard, it will be effective at any time.

Moving Down the Lane to the Low Post

While an offensive system such as the UCLA high post or the UCLA high-low produces the best post-up situations for the post player, many offenses today do not place a player in the post. The reason may be the coach does not have a true big man, or it could also be that his tall players are capable of making the outside shot.

All five players moving, passing, and screening away from the hoop, as well as making occasional basket cuts, is sometimes called "five out." While this system may appear to be looking for a three-point shot, it also creates wonderful post-up opportunities when a player capable of posting up cuts down the lane and down screens for a player close to the basket. The movement is very similar to the down screen mentioned earlier, with the best situation being the slip screen because it catches the defender off guard. This down screen can be made from the guard position or the wing; it is equally effective either way.

Again, the spin move is used but the direction of the spin, clockwise or counterclockwise, depends on where the ball is. For example, if the basketball is on the left wing and the player down screens from the top, he will spin clockwise.

Figure 4-7. Player in the middle of the key, spinning clockwise toward the left wing where the ball is

If the ball is on the right wing, he will spin counterclockwise. If the ball is at the top and the player is on the left wing screening down on the block, he spins counterclockwise. This is identical to the down screen mentioned earlier. When he is on the right side, he will spin clockwise.

The Duck Move

When the ball is not at the low-post player's wing, he must always face the key. The reason is: when he does this, the defender will never front the post. In fact, he will never even begin to move around to front the post, even if his coach has instructed him to do so. It is the defender's nature to assume the post will be moving in the direction he is facing. Maintaining a facing-the-key position is pivotal to a successful sideways stance and also to executing the duck move properly.

A duck move is made when the offensive player moves from outside the lane into the middle of the key to receive the ball from a teammate positioned at the top, either at the high post or the point. The method for getting open is almost identical to that for getting open when cutting across the key, starting with a cross-step baseline followed by the spin, again with the upper back making contact with the defender.

Figure 4-8. Post player faking baseline with right foot, ready for the duck move

Figure 4-9. Post player spinning into the key for the duck move, back against defender and good target, showing the ball at the high post

Scoring

When the player catches the basketball after spinning to get the defender behind him, a quick move must be made. For me, it was the running hook shot (one-foot takeoff a la Kareem Abdul-Jabbar) with either hand. But today, players are using the jump hook (jumping with two feet) very successfully. I favor the running hook because it makes it more difficult to block, as the defender must move laterally and then jump. Either way, the key is to shoot quickly after the catch because the defender has not had time to get set.

A second method of scoring I learned from watching Scottie Pippen. When catching the ball, the player must always catch it in the air and then come down with both feet at the same time. Scottie, when landing with both feet, dropped one of them toward the basket, pivoted, and executed a drop step without needing a dribble. When he was about to catch the ball, his experience allowed him to sense which side the defender was on, and he dropped the leg away from him, where the opening was.

Key Points

- The immediate reverse keeps the defense honest.
- The sideways stance keeps the defender behind the post.
- A juicy target gives the passer confidence.
- The spin move guarantees getting open.

CHAPTER 5

How Do I Teach My Post Player to Seal at the Low Post?

The low-post seal is a counter positioning maneuver used when the post player is fronted, meaning the defender has moved between the offensive post player and the passer in an attempt to prevent the direct pass in. The post player uses his body to seal the defender so he cannot get back behind him. At the moment of the seal, or ideally a second before the seal is completed, the ball is passed from the wing to the high-post area, a better angle from which to enter the ball.

While the seal maneuver is included in the getting open category (addressed in Chapter 4), it is such an important post tool, involves so much detail to execute properly, is so very different than getting open in other areas of the floor, and is such a neglected teaching area (probably the most neglected), I felt the need to devote an entire chapter to it. While some post players are able to get open in most situations, they seem to have great trouble with this one. And, while I am frequently asked by coaches to show how a post player should get open to receive the ball in the low-post area, I am asked how they should seal at least four times as much. Therefore, I was convinced that coaches actually try to teach the seal but are having little success getting any results out of it.

The effectiveness of half-court offense over the course of several games is dependent, in part, on getting the basketball to the post area, not only once in a while, but as an integral part of the offensive system. To win, a team must be able to score close to the basket and from the perimeter. Any team that attempts to accomplish this through dribble penetration alone will rarely win a title. But when the ball is passed to the post (low or high), a defense will collapse to stop the immediate inside score, which opens up inside and outside shooting opportunities as receivers are cutting to the basket and screens on the perimeter are opening up jump shots. When the post is fronted, a defensive retreat will not happen, at least not to the degree it does when the ball is in the post. And defenses will continue to front if they don't have to pay for the tactic. Paying would mean the offense gets the ball to the fronted post for the score. The low-post seal is one of the essential and fundamental maneuvers for the complete offensive post player because, without this threat, the effectiveness of the post player is reduced by half.

This was certainly the case at UCLA when I was a student-athlete there and our center was Bill Walton. Bill was arguably the most complete post player our school ever had, reversing to receive lob passes, getting open with great skill and deception, and being able to efficiently score from the post area almost at will it seemed.

When Bill became eligible for varsity and the season started, it did not take long for opponents to become alarmed at how dangerous UCLA was offensively when Bill had possession of the basketball. They double-teamed him often, sometimes even before he received the ball, zoning the rest of the half-court. That worked for a while until we wised up and began lobbing the ball to Larry Farmer on the weakside. Then they tried fronting Bill, which delighted him (and us) greatly. Bill was highly trained to seal and score, so much so that when he even sensed his defender was moving between him and the ball, he sealed, raising his off-hand toward the basket, and we got him the ball. Once he did that a couple of times, the other team either double-teamed him again, or his defender moved safely behind Bill, which enabled us to continue to use him as a passer and scorer. In other words, without the seal, Bill Walton's offensive effectiveness would have been greatly reduced.

The technique I am going to present for sealing at the low post is exactly what Bill Walton used and what I used in the pros. In fact, it's what Tim Duncan used and what other professional post players use most of the time.

Let's first start by discussing why the seal isn't working for some players. How many times have you seen a post player seal (seemingly open), but the opening is not really there, or more commonly, by the time the ball is repositioned, the opening has closed?

Why the Seal Does Not Work

- The defender is not properly sealed.
- The player cannot maintain the seal.
- The pass is not made at the proper time.
- The pass is not made properly.

The Proper Method of Sealing at the Low Post

The post player has control over the first two points. When the proper method of sealing is employed and the seal is maintained, half the battle is won. With the defender between the passer and the post player, the rest is up to the perimeter passers.

Front vs. Reverse Pivot

The post player will be using a front pivot rather than a reverse or back pivot. Let's discuss the difference. A pivot is almost always a 180-degree turn. The front pivot is called that because the player moves his free foot (as opposed to his pivot foot) forward. The back pivot is called that because the player moves his foot backward.

To explain this better, imagine a player squarely facing a wall. The player is going to use the left foot as the pivot foot, meaning that the left foot remains in contact with the floor at all times while the right foot will swing around, turning the body 180 degrees. When the player uses a front pivot, the right foot will go forward, toward the wall, and swing around. Now the back is toward the wall. When using a back pivot, the right foot will go backward, away from the wall, and swing around. Again, the back is to the wall.

While the back pivot is the best maneuver in some basketball situations (e.g., when receiving the ball at the wing and squaring up for the triple threat), the proper pivot when sealing at the low post is the front pivot. Traditionally, however, the post player is taught to use the back pivot when sealing. Picture the post player positioned on the left side of the key (when looking at the key from the half-court line). Facing the wing, the left foot would be his pivot foot, and the right foot would swing backward and around. The reason the front pivot is the proper move is that, when using the back pivot, the post player loses vision of the basketball and he loses contact with his defender.

Losing Vision

When back pivoting, the player's head turns with the swing foot, which means he is looking at the other side of the half-court before returning his sight to the basketball. Should the basketball be passed while he is turning (e.g., lob pass), which we all have seen happen, a turnover is likely. When front pivoting, the post player's eyes can track the ball no matter where it is located.

That brings up another point, which I will present in the form of a question. From the point of view of the passer, either the wing or the point, is it a safer pass to throw the ball to a post player who is turning his head (back pivot) and has lost vision, or to one who has maintained vision of the ball?

At Duke University, Coach K teaches the fronted post player to direct the ball handler to pass the ball to the free throw line area by pointing at the target area with the free hand (the hand that is not sealing). This is a signal he has sealed and is ready. That gesture must be performed as quickly as possible once the seal has been established. The more the pass is delayed, the more the defender will get back around the offensive player. The back pivot takes too long because the player must first pivot and then point. But when he is using the front pivot, the player can point while sealing.

Losing Contact

When the seal is made and the ball is moved to the free throw line area, the defender becomes stressed as he now knows he is extremely vulnerable; his ploy to prevent the ball from going to the post player is in serious jeopardy. He then begins to move toward the free throw line to get around the post player over the top, or he moves down to get behind him. Because the back pivot causes the post player to lose vision, not only of the basketball but also of his defender, he cannot proactively react to either of these defensive movements and maintain the seal.

However, when front pivoting, the post player keeps contact with the defender and can instantly react to his movements, maintaining the seal longer. In fact, the front pivot enables the post player to actually increase the degree of contact. I have always believed, while effective post defending is reliant on avoiding contact as much as possible, effective offense is dependent on obtaining, maintaining, and even increasing contact. Contact retards defensive adjustments. Such is the case here.

Another reason the front pivot is more effective is that it requires a pivot of fewer degrees, which makes the turn quicker. To make a back pivot in this situation, the player must turn about 180 degrees, sometimes even more. When fronted, the post player is actually almost facing the top of the key; at the least, he is facing the area between the wing and the point. A front pivot requires about a 90-degree turn.

Let's put this all in steps with more detail:
- When fronted, the player faces the top of the key and puts his hip into the defender's backside, maintaining pressure so the defender can't move him back. He lifts his hands and elbows above the defender's shoulders to prepare for the seal and to avoid the push-off call.
- When it is apparent that the ball will not be passed into the post from the wing, and before the ball is passed to the top of the key, the player thrusts the hand closest to the defender across his neck area and toward the top of the key and maintains strong contact on his neck and upper back with the upper arm. He keeps that arm straight, locked, and pointing toward the top of the key.

Figure 5-1. Player shooting arm past defender, no leg yet

- Almost simultaneously, the player steps with the leg closest to the defender, toward the top of the key, directly under the outstretched arm, and moves his hip into the defender's backside. He increases pressure and keeps facing the top of the key. The ball should be on its way to the high post at this point.

Figure 5-2. Player with leg past defender and arm shooting past defender's neck

- The player maintains the complete seal by sliding with the defender as he moves up the side of the lane, while the ball is passed to the top. The ball should be on its way to the point or high post.
- The player presents a target toward the middle of the key area with the hand that is not sealing.
- The player aggressively leaves to get the ball, only after the ball has been released by the passer and is almost to the area where he wants to catch it. In other words, he should maintain the seal as long as possible. A general rule is: the player should release the seal when the ball is over his head.
  - ✓ The player should give the defender zero chance of an interception.
  - ✓ The player should go get the ball like it was a rebound.
  - ✓ The player should use the quick running hook or a drop step power move to score. This will depend on where he is when receiving the ball.

Final Words

When the pass is made from the top into the key to the player who has sealed, most coaches teach the player to immediately elevate and shoot the jump hook shot. That is, most definitely, an option and a good one. But it is only one option. I say, why limit the player? If he is taught to come to a jump stop with both feet touching down simultaneously, there are more options, depending on how the defender is positioned. If he is out of position completely, the player can continue with a one-footed elevation for the lay-up or short hook shot, for example. Dribbling the basketball is to be avoided as it slows the move down and increases the chances of a turnover.

Remember, although it is ideal for the player to catch the basketball close to the basket, in most cases he will catch it anywhere from 6 to 10 feet out. Taking the long drop step toward the backboard and using the running hook not only trims down the distance to the hoop, it separates the shooter from the defender, resulting in a shot that is not challenged (the jump hook will be challenged). The separation and penetration will also result in better offensive rebounding position should the shot be missed.

The turnaround jump shot may be the best option for the player who has a nice touch. I once saw a player fake the jump shot and execute an up-and-under (fake and step past the faked defender and to the basket) beautifully.

Key Points

- When fronted, the player should turn sideways to get leverage with his hip.
- The player should front pivot.
- The player should shoot his arm and leg past the defender and create strong contact.
- The player should keep the defender sealed with footwork.
- The player should leave to get the ball after it is passed.

CHAPTER 6
How Can I Teach the Drop Step?

When I go out of town on vacation, I almost always make arrangements with the local high school to work with their post players for a couple of hours. Some people think I'm crazy, but I just can't help myself. The thought of some unskilled post players needing a little help (which is always the case), while I'm in town, with the ability to teach them the basics and to motivate them to learn the rest of post play, is almost unbearable. How could it be that I don't help these wonderful student-athletes, when as a freshman at Cypress College, my first year of basketball, Tom Lubin and Don Johnson went out of their way to teach me how to play in the post? I feel more than compelled to do the same, even when on vacation on the Big Island in Hawaii, where I have conducted four post clinics, free of charge. When I was making plans with the principal of that school, who had been a basketball coach himself, he asked me to teach getting open, rebounding, and especially the drop step.

The principal deemed the drop step to be the primary move for low-post play, and he was not alone. From my experience, most coaches (over 90 percent) teach it. But that is an erroneous statement. As Coach Wooden often said, "We can only say we have 'taught' when the student has learned," and when I watch high school basketball today, I do not see the drop step used much at all, and when it is, there are no productive results. So what we have are coaches teaching the drop step in practice and the players rarely applying it in games. Why is that?

I have to admit: I never used the classic drop step in college or the pros. I didn't use it because it didn't work. When initiating the move with the baseline leg dropping toward the basket, my opponent, the same size and weight as me, simply bumped me, and I ended up not under the basket, which was the plan, but under the backboard. Instead, I used the spin move, the spall (which is discussed in Chapter 8). The reason I didn't use the drop step is not because it's not effective; it's because I didn't know the keys to pulling it off successfully. Those keys I learned long after retiring from basketball. Had I known them then, I would certainly have used the drop step on occasion.

My epiphany came while conducting one of my "Play Post Like the Pros" post player clinics in Missouri. In my clinics, after warming the players up, I have them go one-on-one in the post so I can observe and evaluate present offensive post skills. Every player had to try to score against every other player in the clinic. One player, about 6'5" and

210 pounds, was particularly effective using the drop step, even though every defender knew that's what he wanted to do. Where I had, up to that point, discounted and discarded the drop step as a usable low-post move, my curiosity was awakened, and I wanted to know how this player was able to use the move so effectively. In the clinic, there were jump shooters and jump hook shooters, some pretty good, but none of them was able to score so easily as this player. In this chapter, I reveal his secrets, and I have been teaching this method ever since with much success.

The 45-Degree Angle

Most post players, when trying to make the drop step move, begin too close to the baseline. Therefore, when they make the drop step move, they end up under the backboard rather than in front of it for the score. Think of the 45-degree angle. The drop step move must be made about 45 degrees to the plane of the backboard. The lower (i.e., the closer to the baseline) the player begins the move, the more difficult it is to get in front of the backboard where the high-percentage lay-up can be made.

Figure 6-1. Offensive post player, too close to baseline, and defender on the side

Figure 6-2. Offensive post player, 45-degree angle to backboard, and defender behind

Of course, in order for the post player to receive the ball in the proper position, the passer must be positioned at about a 45-degree angle as well. Some offenses have a shooter run the baseline, use the post as a screen, and move to the three-point line in the corner for the shot. In order to receive a pass from that player, should his shot not be available, the post, in order to keep the defender behind him, must be positioned on the line between the ball and the basket, a rather low position, which eliminates the use of the drop step. If, in this situation, with the ball close to the baseline, the post player is positioned up the lane at the 45-degree angle, the chances for a successful pass are reduced as the defender usually moves around the post player on the baseline side, in a very good position to make a steal or deflection. For the defender, there is very little risk. Therefore, ideally, for the post to use the drop step, the pass to the post must be made from the same 45-degree angle or somewhere close to that.

By the way, that higher position improves the angle for going across the key for the hook shot or jump hook; if the player makes a move across the key from too low a position, he will naturally be moving away from the basket; the distance between the player and the basket increases as the maneuver matures, usually reducing the shooting percentage. However, when the player starts higher up and makes the move for the running hook or jump hook, he can maintain the distance or even decrease it. With few exceptions, scoring success at the low post increases when the player makes the move toward the hoop.

Deception: A Key to the Successful Drop Step

According to John Wooden, deception is key to team scoring. When the defense is in tune with what the offense is trying to do and what particular shot the offense is attempting to get, its anticipation of ball movement will allow it to put pressure on every pass. By nature, because the offense is usually a little ahead of the defense, defenders anticipate the next move and lean a little (sometimes a lot) in that direction, particularly when an upcoming pass is anticipated and obvious. Good offense should take advantage of that. Effective defenses foresee things, but productive offenses get the defenses looking in the wrong direction, and then quickly move the ball to the ignored shooters, usually on the weakside.

A magician's success with card tricks is completely dependent on maneuvers such as sleight of hand and misdirection. The concept is to point the audience in one direction, while cards are being switched where they are not looking. UCLA used to get the ball to Kareem just when it looked like the play was going to another player on the other side of the half-court. In an instant, the ball was reversed into Kareem's hands and up went the Skyhook, and we knew that was "money."

For example, Johnny Green, a big guard for UCLA during the early 1960s, received the ball on the wing and passed it back out to the point. Green then casually moved down to the low post. With screening occurring on the side away from Green, and the point looking that direction, the defense, including Green's defender, naturally moved over. The point faked a pass to the screen area, took one dribble back toward Green, who had button-hooked at the post to have his defender sealed, and delivered the ball. It was almost a guaranteed score.

Offensive post play is not different; deception is key to getting the high-percentage shot, the shot you really want to take. The shot I always wanted was the hook shot, either across the key from the left side or the baseline hook from the right. But in professional basketball, all of us were well-scouted. The other team often knew us better than we knew ourselves. (Players with only one move never make it in the NBA.) So, I faked to the other side, moving the defender over, and made my favorite move. A fake pass also worked on occasion.

The Fake

With that in mind, in order to open up the baseline for the drop step, the player must fake to the middle and quickly reverse the other way. But the fake must be executed without a dribble because that takes too long. By the time the player reverses, the defender will cut him off. The fake is made by moving the head toward the middle (looking across the key) and, most important, moving the ball in that direction as well, still keeping it close to the body. It's almost like trying to hand the ball to the defender. "Here you go. Take it!" The defender must see the ball. Equally important, when faking, the player reclines so the upper back will make contact with the defender. We will see the importance of this later.

The Drop Step Seal

At exactly the same time as the fake, the leg closest to the baseline (the drop step leg) goes back past the defender as far as possible and makes contact with the floor. It is important to know that the fake and the step happen as one motion. If the fake is done properly, the body actually torques, which is what will wind the player up for the quick uncoiling move. If it is convincing, the fake will move the defender a little toward the middle, or if he is smart and doesn't buy the counterfeit, he will at least be frozen in his place.

Moving Into Position

The drop step is the most difficult low-post move to execute properly. That is why few have mastered it. But it can be the most difficult move to defend. Success is dependent on details, three to be exact.

- *Turn and roll off the chest:* While maintaining upper back contact with the defender, the player turns toward the baseline, rolling off the defender's chest and toward the basket. At the end of this move, the inside shoulder will be in contact with the defender, and the player's head will be between the defender's head and the basket area. To illustrate, when rolling, the head moves directly toward the basket. Most players move their head toward the baseline.
- *Lower upper body:* While turning, the player begins to lower the upper body. (He does not lean forward; he keeps contact with the back).

Figure 6-3. While turning, the player maintains upper body contact.

- *Dribble and gather:* The player takes one dribble with two hands between the feet ("crab dribble") and hops with both feet toward the basket, gathering the body into a balanced position to score.

Figure 6-4. After the dribble, the player gathers the body into a balanced position to score.

The Importance of Upper Back Contact

Addressing the upper back contact again is important because this will be the most difficult component to teach, as it will most likely be new to the player. Most players have been trained to contact the opponent's legs with their backsides (a nice term for "butt"). Why make contact with the upper back rather than the backside? The upper back seal moves the defender's head back, preventing him from catching up. You see, a defender cannot move his feet unless the head moves first. On the contrary, contact with the backside to the defender's legs leaves the defender's head free. A second reason is, because this position has the offensive post already leaning in the direction of the basket, the move to the basket will be quicker and more effective.

Figure 6-5. Upper back contact

Additional Applications

When the defender is playing close enough and to the high side, the jump stop drop step can be most effective. At the moment the ball is received, the player makes a jump stop with the baseline leg dropping toward the basket and past the defender's legs. If the player is close enough to the basket, the score can be made without the dribble.

Figure 6-6. Jump stop drop step

The drop step move is not limited to the low post; it can be used any time an offensive player has his back to the defense. When the player is positioned at the high post, with the back to the basket and the defender close behind, it can be used to initiate a drive to the basket. One UCLA offense option is called the side-post game. The post player comes to the weakside elbow and receives the ball from the point. After passing, the point heads directly to the post player and cuts off him to the basket, on one side or the other, depending on how his defender is playing him. At any point of the play, the post can make his fake, drop step, and drive to the basket. But it is most effective at the moment the cutter passes by. A fake handoff will most certainly move the post defender, opening up a lane to drop step and drive.

Key Points

- The player should maintain upper back contact.
- The player should make a convincing fake to the middle while dropping the leg around the defender and toward the basket.
- The player should roll off the defender, keeping contact with his upper back to seal.
- The player should sit on the defender's leg to immobilize him.

CHAPTER 7
How Do I Teach the Fundamentals of Post Play?

What Are Fundamentals?

The fundamentals of basketball are the basics and rudiments of the game. We can also say they are the bare bones of the game. Passing, cutting, pivoting, and shooting are some of those fundamentals. All individual movements or actions seen in a basketball game (e.g., pick and roll, driving to the basket, rebounding, and jump shooting) are complex maneuvers that can be broken down into fundamentals that are combined back to back. For example, the lay-up maneuver is composed of two fundamentals: dribbling and shooting. The offensive rebound maneuver consists of three fundamentals: cutting, pivoting, and jumping.

Coach Wooden and Fundamentals

Coach Wooden taught the fundamentals of basketball better than most coaches, perhaps better than all college coaches. This was evident in the way UCLA played basketball, particularly in how we executed plays on both ends of the court, quickly and under complete control. The quick and proper execution of plays on both ends of the court was the signature of UCLA basketball under Coach Wooden. There was nothing fancy about the way we did things; we just did whatever needed to be done with leanness and quickness, and we were never in a hurry. The fundamentals were drilled daily for the entire season with the goal of bringing us to automaticity. Automaticity is achieved when the fundamentals are executed properly and quickly with no conscious thought. A state of automaticity allows a player and a team to concentrate on the game, rather than execution. It can only be obtained through practice.

"But," you say, "I teach the fundamentals too." Most coaches today can say they teach the fundamentals, but if it were possible for them to watch our UCLA practices, they would soon come to the realization that they do not teach the basics with the attention to detail and to the extent Coach Wooden did. I have observed numerous high school basketball practices, and there are few coaches who get close to Coach Wooden in this area. Moreover, if Coach Wooden believed in the priority of the fundamentals at the college level, where most of us were All-Americans, how much more important is it at the lower levels? Following are most of the fundamental exercises we did at UCLA every single day. It took at least one-sixth of the two-hour practice.

The First 20 Minutes of a UCLA Practice

Change of Pace, Change of Direction

- Full-court cutting
- Accelerating when changing directions
- Hands at shoulder height
- Head directly above the midpoint between the feet
- All joints flexed and relaxed

Defensive Sliding With No Offense, Basic

- Changing directions to guard the imaginary dribbler
- Balanced at all times
- Feet never coming completely together
- Hands at waist level to guard the dribble, but elbows close to the sides so as not to extend too much or balance will be compromised and changing direction quickly will be hindered and slowed

Defensive Sliding With No Offense, Imaginary Catch-Up

- This drill is the same as the basic version, but when changing direction, the defender sprints to catch up with the imaginary offensive player who has beaten him with the dribble. The defender must block his path and get back on balance quickly. Per Coach Wooden, this was one of his best methods for teaching balance. He said, "To learn balance, you must get off balance and regain it."

One-on-One Full-Court, No Basketball, No Beating the Defender

- The offensive man uses change of pace and change of direction while the defender uses defensive sliding. The offensive man tests the balance of the defender by making sharp and non-telegraphed cuts. At this point, he does not try to beat the defender. Players change offense to defense at half-court.

One-on-One Full Court, No Basketball, Then Basketball, Beating the Defender

- The offensive man, when getting the defender off balance, tries to sprint past him. The defender outsprints the dribbler, blocks his path down the court, and resumes balance to guard. Note: When he is blocking the path of the dribbler, the defender must not be too close to him or he'll get beaten again. He must be about two arm lengths away. Bill Walton and I had fun doing this drill. At first, the cutter had no basketball. Next, he dribbled.

Imaginary Jump Shooting

- The entire team stands in a group, arm's length apart, facing the coach. On the coach's whistle, they jump and execute the jump shot.

Details

- Players are on balance with feet a little wider than the shoulders, head directly above the midpoint between the two feet, chin up, shooting elbow above the knee, back straight, and a wrinkle in the shooting wrist.
- Players should rise quickly.
- While elevating, the elbow keeps moving up until the release. This eliminates the two-count shot and provides the quick release. Coach believed, "You shoot by the man, not over him." An imaginary ball is released just before the peak of the jump. This allows the body to put momentum into the basketball, resulting in a better touch. Shooting is almost effortless when releasing the ball while rising.
- The elbow should be above the ear with fingers pointed down to the floor after release.
- The hand should be brought down on the same path as it went up, as if a film was run in reverse. This prevents the elbow from falling at release, which is the cause for the flat shot. The jump shot is a lift, not a push.

Imaginary Rebounding, Boxing Out

- In pairs, players face each other about arm's length apart. The offensive player makes a move to his right. The defender blocks his path and jumps for the imaginary rebound, coming down with the imaginary ball and making the imaginary outlet pass. They do the same drill with the cutter going the other way.

Details

- The defender steps toward the cutter to block his path, touching the cutter's chest with the open hand. In other words, he simply gets in his way.
- The defender goes to get the rebound. There is no holding the man when blocking him out. It's a hit and go. Many rebounds are lost by doing a wonderful job blocking out and failing to go get the ball.

Note: On the left side of the basket, for example, with the cutter about 10 or so feet from the basket, the defender is in the open stance with his right hand close to the cutter. If the cutter goes across the key, the defender steps in his path with the right foot. If the cutter goes baseline, the defender makes a reverse pivot and steps in his path. Many coaches would teach the reverse pivot for blocking the cut across the key, but Coach Wooden's method makes more sense as it keeps the defender's eyes to the court and on the ball.

Imaginary Rebounding, Offense

This drill is the same as the boxing out drill, but the offensive player gets by the defender. The player fakes one way, shoots the open hand past the defender's neck and toward the desired spot, and steps through with the inside foot, sealing and holding.

Although we did not learn this at UCLA, I would add the step and spin. The offensive player steps with the right foot across his body, for example, toward the left side of the defender, and spins/rolls off him to the right and toward the basket. This move is virtually unstoppable.

Anti-Over Jumping

Jumping for height is not enough to secure the ball. Players must have proper timing and have their hands ready to snatch the basketball. Three players are at the basket, two in on one side (the first one has the basketball) and one on the other side. The player with the ball throws the ball off the board to the other side of the basket, where the single player is positioned. The player that threw the ball moves behind the single player on the other side, taking the route back into the court, not to the baseline. While in the air and at the top of his jump, the single player grabs the ball with both hands and sends it to the other side, where there is now a single player. Then he moves behind that player, and so on and so forth. It looks like a weave. The goal is to get 10 touches and, on the tenth, the player scores.

Details

- Hands are kept at shoulder height at all times except when rebounding.
- Quick sprints are taken to get in position on the other side of the basket.

Variation

- One-hand tipping should be used rather than grabbing the ball with both hands.

Rebound Pass-Out Drill

This half-court passing drill using four players is difficult to describe without video or demonstration. The ball is passed from the point to the wing, passed back to the point who has cut into the key (give and go), thrown up on the board by the point and rebounded, passed back to the same wing, who has cut toward half-court and come back to get open (overhead pass or whatever the coach designates), and passed back to the new point (the player who was waiting behind the original point). Then the operation switches to the other side of the half-court. It is a give and go followed by a rebound pass-out.

Dribbling, Pivot, and Passing Drill

Players set up in four lines across the baseline, with three players in each line behind the baseline, facing the other side of the court. The first player in each line has a basketball. On the whistle, the first player dribbles with his right hand, sprints to the free throw line extended, and comes to a sudden jump stop on balance, chinning the ball. On the next whistle, he makes an inside pivot to his left, now facing the other players. On the next whistle, he makes a pass to the first player in line. (The coach decides what pass he wants worked on, which he can change during the drill.) Then, he makes a quick change-of-pace and change-of-direction move toward the baseline and continues to the back of the line. As he is about to cross the baseline, the whistle blows for the next player to begin.

Variations

- Different passes
- Dribbles with the other hand
- Pivots the other way
- Front pivots rather than reverse (although Coach Wooden taught only the reverse pivot)

Weaves, Full-Court

This drill starts with three players, one under the basket and the others on the wings at one end of the court. The player in the middle has the ball. He passes to one side and goes behind that player and back to the middle. The player with the ball passes to the other wing, who has cut into the middle of the court, and so on and so forth. The last man scores the basket. Then, the same drill is repeated with five players. The emphasis should be on quick passing, jump stops, and proper footwork to prevent traveling. The receiver always comes to a jump stop. This drill, of course, is also a good conditioning drill.

Variation

- Three-man tight weave: This drill is the same as the first, but the three players weave extremely close to each other, even to the point of sometimes touching, all the way down the court. The passes are simply little throw-ups or handoffs where the ball is lifted about five inches or so with both hands so the next player can grab it. In our offense, we had some situations where we used this pass (e.g., side-post game).

Various Fast Break Drills

For about 5 to 10 minutes, we did fast break drills. They were three-man drills, with one player throwing the ball on the backboard, rebounding it, and starting the fast break with the outlet pass, and five-man drills, where we practiced the many options of our breaking system.

Details Win Championships

We did every one of these drills, or a variation thereof, every single day, all season. Some coaches may claim to do the same, but from my experience, as the season progresses, less time is given to fundamentals, which are replaced by more scrimmaging. Coach Wooden was fully engaged during fundamentals instruction; he corrected every error and insisted we execute properly. As we improved execution, he commanded us to pick up the pace. The goal was quick and proper execution of the basics.

Most coaches do not do this, but rather, they call out the name of the drill and believe the drill itself will teach. This is a very big mistake. While the drill is going on, they talk among themselves. Coach Wooden and his assistants were pacing up and down the floor, catching every mistake we were making, and yelling out corrections like, "Back straight, elbows tucked in, wrinkle in the wrist, move to the other side more quickly!" Ladies and gentlemen, this is how UCLA hardly ever lost a game; we didn't beat ourselves because we didn't throw the ball away, miss the open shot, miss a rebound, or dribble the ball off our feet at the end of games. Oh, some other teams may have beaten us, but we never beat ourselves by making fundamental mistakes.

Not Enough Time to Thoroughly Teach Fundamentals

Each season, the curriculum is extensive, sometimes even daunting. There is half-court offense against a zone, half-court offense against a man-to-man, breaking the full-court press, breaking the three-quarter-court press, breaking the half-court press, out-of-bounds plays, time and score situations, man-to-man half-court defense, full-court defense, special defenses, free throws, conditioning, team play, and fundamentals. That's a lot, and coaches today don't have as much practice time because the gymnasium must be shared equally with the JV and freshman teams, not to mention the women's teams and other sports such as volleyball. It is tough to teach everything in one season.

But there is good news: giving proper time to teaching fundamentals actually saves time. Teams that are fundamentally sound learn new things more quickly because they can execute; no additional time is necessary to correct an errant pass, cut, or shot. Like Coach Wooden said, "If you don't have time to do it right, when will you have time to do it over?" He had a fetish for saving time and a hatred for wasting it. As you already know, he spent at least one-sixth of practice, every day, teaching the basics in detail.

Obviously, for him, that was not a waste of time. Why? Because Coach believed that when you drill in the fundamentals of basketball, you will save time teaching the rest of the game. Again, when players become skilled dribblers, passers, and shooters, for example, they will learn to execute an offensive play in a fraction of the time.

Simply running rebound drills, for example, doesn't improve rebounding as quickly as teaching the basics first and then putting them to the test in competition. When I was a coach, my team was soft on the boards, and I was tempted to run rebounding drills by throwing the ball up on the glass and having my guys box out and race for the rebound to make them tougher. I thought all they needed to get tough was to battle, but I was wrong; they needed technique first. Improved skill breeds improved confidence, which, in turn, results in increased aggressiveness. When I began teaching the basics, I found that they got tougher at boxing out because the technique was sounder, and the repetition resulted in quicker execution. I found they got tough maneuvering to the offensive boards for the same reason. Running competitive drills before teaching fundamentals was putting the cart before the horse. This was a grave mistake of mine and of many young coaches.

How to Develop Post Fundamentals

Finally, we have arrived at the question: How do I teach the fundamentals of post play? My objective for the lengthy prologue is to help convince you that the quickest, most effective, and most long-lasting method for developing the novice post player is to give plenty of season-long time and attention to developing the foundation.

Coach Wooden taught his post players the fundamentals as if we knew nothing and had no foundation, even though we were All-Americans. How much more, then, should high school coaches properly and exhaustively teach those basic building blocks of the individual post game? In fact, by Coach's standards, most of us had mediocre foundations at best. Just because a player wins a high school championship or receives honors doesn't mean he is fundamentally ready for college play. And the NBA all-time roster is saturated with players who, based on their talent and lower-level success, promised to become superstars, but due to a weak foundation, topped out as good players.

Coach Wooden taught the posts the fundamentals at three levels: general fundamentals, small-group teaching, and individual attention.

General Fundamentals

First, the post players did the same basic fundamental drills the guards and forwards were asked to do. They are listed earlier in this chapter. Post play, like forward or guard play, requires cutting, sliding, pivoting, jumping, passing, and running. At UCLA, everyone did all of those exercises. As it turns out, except for post defense and some of the shooting basics that were specific to post offense (e.g., running hooks, jump hooks, reverse lay-ups), the fundamentals for post play were covered in the basic drills (pivoting, jump stops, blocking out, getting around the block-out, and passing).

Fundamentals in Small-Group Teaching

With guards, forwards, and centers at different baskets, we worked on position-specific fundamentals and put them to the test as they were applied to the offensive and defensive plays to be learned. In other words, we were put into competition to evaluate how well the basics were working. During competition, the coaches corrected the errors in fundamentals and kept notes to be used when planning the following practices.

For example, Bill Walton and I worked on offensive low-post moves with one of the assistant coaches, Gary Cunningham. Footwork, shooting, and pivoting were the major focus. This was done in three stages. First we executed the move with no defense, second against nominal defense, and third against full defense. All the while, Coach Cunningham was correcting fundamental mistakes that were causing failure to execute properly and quickly.

The guards, at another basket, may have been working on the UCLA cut, the guard reverse, or the very effective side-post game. Again, the three stages were used, and most of the time, the work moved from the right side of the basket to the left and back and forth.

Small-group teaching was given at least 20 minutes, so you could say we spent 40 minutes, or one-third of practice, on fundamentals, the first 20 on developing them in isolation as corrections were made, and the second 20 on testing them in game situations.

Individual Attention

At UCLA, practice was never longer than two and a half hours. The first half hour was always reserved for Coach and his assistants working with individuals, or two or three players at most, on certain things. It may have been free throws, dribbling, shooting, or anything else. For example, Ralph Drollinger needed lots of work with his outlet pass and received plenty of instruction before practice. During that first half hour, Coach and his assistants taught fundamentals to those players that needed extra instruction. They also taught other things that needed work, such as components of the full-court press or two-guard tandem defense (e.g., Andre McCarter and Pete Trgovich).

During small groups, the fundamentals were analyzed and reinforced. During general fundamentals, they were taught in detail to the group. Before practice, players received individual attention and lots of extra repetition. Do you get the point? It's all about the fundamentals, and that's why skill is a major block in what Coach called the "heart" of the Pyramid of Success.

What were the fundamentals for post play that we needed work on, beyond the general fundamentals? That depended on what each post player did in games. Bill Walton needed to learn jump stops and pivots more than Kareem Abdul-Jabbar because Bill came to the high post often to provide backdoor pass relief for the wings. Post players needed teaching of offensive moves, defensive moves at the low post and perhaps the high post, offensive rebounding maneuvers, blocking out, jumping/ rebounding, and blocking shots.

The Six Shots in the Post

Regardless of the individual needs of each player, all post players must be fully skilled at executing the six shots in the post with the right hand and the left hand.

Running Hook

The player jumps off one leg and shoots with the opposite hand. The ball is released with the arm completely straight and just a little behind the head to create space between the ball and the defender. Follow-through is with the wrist and with the entire arm coming down toward the basket.

Figure 7-1. Running hook

Jump Hook

This shot uses the same action as the running hook, but the player jumps off two feet. The ball is released before the top of the jump for quickness (shooting by the defender, not over him) and momentum.

Figure 7-2. Jump hook

Mikan Drill

The player again uses the same action as the running hook, but with short bank shots.

Figure 7-3. Mikan drill

Bank Jump Shots

The player releases the ball before the top of the jump, again to shoot by the defender.

Figure 7-4. Bank jump shots

Reverse Lay-Up, Inside Hand

The player shoots with the hand closest to the basket. He does not need to spin the ball; proper release produces natural spin because of how the ball is positioned in the hand.

Figure 7-5. Reverse lay-up, inside hand

Reverse Lay-Up, Outside Hand

The player shoots with the hand farthest away from the basket. This time, some spin will be needed. Mastery of this shot will take some repetition, particularly with the non-dominant hand.

Figure 7-6. Reverse lay-up, outside hand

To practice the six shots in one drill, the player starts with the running hook, alternating right- and left-hand shots until 10 are made. Then he moves to the jump hook and so on and so forth. When he makes 60 shots (10 of each shot), the clock stops. Next time, the player tries to improve his time. My best was 2 minutes and 15 seconds.

The Job Breakdown Sheet (JBS)

Training Within Industry (TWI) was a WWII program within the U.S. War Manpower Commission, with the mission to help factories that were given government contracts to manufacture war-related materials more quickly so our troops overseas would have replenishment. Because some of their young employees were called off to war, they were usually low on personnel, not to mention they needed more employees than normal because of the increased demand. So there was a definite challenge; they hired many untrained people (e.g., Rosie the Riveter).

In time, TWI created three main programs designed to train the factory manager to train the supervisors, who would, in turn, train the workers. Those three main programs were: How to Instruct, How to Improve Things, and How to Build Relationships. By the end of the war, over 1.6 million workers in over 1600 plants had received certification.

It has been said that TWI was a major reason for our WWII success because it met its mission; the production and export of food, materials, weapons, and ammunition was greatly increased.

One of the tools TWI created in the How to Instruct program was the Job Breakdown Sheet (JBS). The JBS provided the supervisor with the steps for each job, the important points (key points) for each step that enabled the worker to do the job properly and quickly, and the reasons for each key point. Every time a worker was being trained, the supervisor taught using the JBS. Because the JBS contained all the information needed to train a worker properly, supervisors were able to decrease training time sometimes thirtyfold. Training a lens grinder, for example, which previously took months, took only a few weeks when using the JBS.

Figure 7-7 is an example of a basketball JBS. I use the JBS every time I teach basketball players and have helped some coaches use them during practice. They report

#	Important Steps	Key Points	Reasons
1	Preparation	• Receive the ball before approaching the free throw line • Feet shoulder-width apart • Stand just behind the line • Shooting arm perpendicular to backboard	• Makes routine more consistent • Balance • Avoid infraction, shortest distance to hoop • Increases accuracy should the ball hit the rim
2	Shooting	• Knees slightly bent, all joints flexed and relaxed • Shooting elbow directly above knee • Wrist cocked, wrinkle in wrist • Chin up • Dribble the ball a few times • Start shot with knees, then elbow, and then hand—chain reaction • Finish with elbow above the ear • Follow through with fingers to the floor (reach in the peach basket) • Hold position for two seconds after release	• Limits moving parts • Limits moving parts • Limits moving parts • Balance • Get a feel for the ball • Relieves the arm from doing too much • Makes the shot a lift, not a push • Puts backspin on the ball for touch • Eliminates elbow dropping during shot
Note: For multiple consecutive free throws, if the first one is made, the player should stay at the free throw line. If it is missed, the player should step back and go through all the key points.			

Figure 7-7. Job Breakdown Sheet for shooting the free throw

the same findings the factories did; it saved time and the instruction was thorough and learning lasted. For the War Manpower Commission, saving time on training meant increased production, which meant our men overseas received what they needed to win the war. For the sports coach, saving time on teaching each skill means more teaching per practice, which translates into increased preparedness for games.

Key Points

- Taking the time to teach fundamentals is worth the investment. It saves time in the long run.
- The details of the fundamentals must be taught.
- Correct all errors so the players get repetition in the proper method.
- Teach general fundamentals to the entire team.
- Teach position-specific fundamentals in small groups.
- Provide extra time and repetition in the fundamentals during the first part of practice.
- Create and use a Job Breakdown Sheet for every fundamental and for every drill.

CHAPTER 8

What Post Moves Should I Teach My Post Player?

Julius Erving had his running leap to the rim for the dunk; Jerry West his clutch 17-foot jump shot; Elgin Baylor the spinning reverse lay-up as he hung in the air for what seemed eternity; Sam Jones the patented bank shot; Hakeem Olajuwon his unstoppable right-handed jump hook; Bill Walton the deadly and lightning-quick turnaround jump shot from the block; and Michael Jordan his acrobatic finishing shots, which thrilled the crowd and demoralized the opponents. But there has never, never been a weapon in the game of basketball like Kareem Abdul-Jabbar's Skyhook. (That's right; I'm capitalizing it because that shot is the only one that deserves it.) Without question, the Skyhook is the greatest single offensive weapon this game has ever seen.

The Skyhook was also the quickest move in the game, from step to release. Once Kareem picked up his dribble and began the final part of the maneuver, it was one long step and, in less than one second, the ball was above the rim, clenched in his huge meat hook-like right hand, and on its way to the basket, most of the time before the defender even thought about jumping to challenge it.

We can learn two things from Kareem about what makes an effective offensive post move. First, he used a move that was perfectly suited for his abilities. Second, he found ways to use the shot almost exclusively, using the counter move as a threat and only when absolutely necessary. From those two points, we learn that the post player doesn't need 10 moves; he needs one high-percentage shot that he can use almost all the time, with one counter to keep the defense honest.

Kareem Abdul-Jabbar's Custom-Made Move

Kareem Abdul-Jabbar was exceptionally agile, incredibly quick, and extremely long, as they say, with a reach (standing flat-footed) that came about three inches shy of the rim. His mobility empowered him to take a big step past the defender and then quickly rise with the ball, most of the time before the defender was able to jump and challenge it. Go online and find pictures of Kareem shooting the Skyhook. In almost every photo, you will see Kareem in the air and the defender still on the floor. It was the perfect shot for him. The Skyhook was custom made for him (or Kareem was custom made for the Skyhook) because he was quick and long.

Figure 8-1. Kareem shooting Skyhook with defender not challenging

Abdul-Jabbar entered the NBA as a member of the Milwaukee Bucks when the great 7'1" Wilt Chamberlain was in the twilight of his career. But Chamberlain still had a vertical jump that could get his hand close to the top of the backboard, enough to block Kareem's Skyhook. When playing Kareem, Wilt had one thing in his competitive mind: to get to that shot just once and swat it down the court. He did it once; I saw it on TV. But most of the time he was too late and the ball swished through the net. Kareem's shot was so quick, by the time Wilt got his hand two feet over the rim to block it, the scorekeeper had already added two points for the Bucks. John Wooden had trained Kareem (Lewis Alcindor at that time) to "shoot the ball past the defender, not over him."

All over the United States, at this very moment, coaches are teaching (not forcing) their post players to use only power moves across the key and to the baseline, baseline drop steps for lay-ups, and drop steps across the key for jump hooks (jumping with two feet). Why? It is because that's all the coaches know. Is the jump hook the right shot for every post player? Imagine a 6'6", 180-pound player trying to outmuscle taller and heavier players to the baseline, or shoot jump hooks over a player four inches taller. It doesn't make sense, right? The moves these coaches are teaching are basic, general moves they believe all post players should use. In most cases, these maneuvers are not placing the post players in a position for success.

Recently, I worked with three high school post players in California. One was 14 years old, 6'8", and physically mature beyond his years. Another was 13, thin, and much weaker. When I asked the 13-year-old to try to score against the 14-year-old, he tried to shoot jump hooks over him in the middle of the key. Every shot he took was swatted to half-court. I asked him, "How is that working for you?" He said, "Not too good." I had him try it again with the same discouraging results. He didn't know any better because he was doing what he was taught. He had never stopped to think, *There must be a better way.* Perhaps he was thinking, *Maybe I'm not shooting it high enough, or I need a quicker release.* When I told him to take one more step past the defender and launch a little Skyhook, the ball was in the basket before the 14-year-old could get off the ground.

But the Skyhook, as effective as it was for Kareem, may not be the most effective shot for some post players. We need to help each post player develop a primary move that takes advantage of his body type and abilities. What if John Wooden had insisted Kareem use turnaround jump shots? Crazy. The opposing coaches would have loved it and would have sent Coach thank-you notes for having Kareem shoot from 10 feet out rather than closer to the basket. But Coach Wooden didn't receive one note of appreciation from his rivals because Abdul-Jabbar had a custom-made move that went to the hoop and was quicker than the shortest time span known to man—the lapse between when the traffic light turns green and the guy in the car behind you beeps his horn.

One Dominant Move

On October 18, 1969, the Milwaukee Bucks hosted the Detroit Pistons. It was Kareem Abdul-Jabbar's first professional game. The world was watching to see how he would do professionally, but equally as important, how he would do against one of the best centers of the time, Walter Jones Bellamy. Bellamy was 6'11", strong, agile, with a very good touch on the basketball. On his way to 29 points, Kareem used drop steps, turnaround jumpers, and the Skyhook, and probably another move or two.

At UCLA, he didn't use half of what he took out of his shooting bag that night; I had no idea he had that extensive an arsenal. Perhaps he was trying to show the world his entire repertoire. All I do know is: it was an impressive debut and exhibition of an extremely complete offensive post game.

But the Kareem Abdul-Jabbar in his later years was much different. Almost exclusively, he used the Skyhook, with an occasional drop step or turnaround jump shot. Somewhere early in his career, he leaned down his repertoire to one move—the Skyhook—and a counter move or two. The Skyhook became his dominant move. It was virtually unstoppable. He was probably thinking, *Why not use it all the time?*

Although Kareem also had the baseline drop step, when he got the ball and looked for his move, he was hell-bent on shooting that hook. He knew every defender he faced was trying to find a way to prevent him from using that weapon, and he was so darned competitive that, most of the time, he found a way to shoot that shot regardless of the determination and tactics of the defender. It's almost like, had he allowed them to take the Skyhook away, he would have plunged into a depressive identity crisis. Kareem was the Skyhook, and the Skyhook was Kareem. There was no option; he just had to use it, and he found ways to pull it off.

When the opponents realized Kareem's signature move was the right-handed Skyhook across the key, they tried to take it away by allowing him to catch the ball on the other side of the key (the right side when facing the backboard from the point). Their thinking was that, from that position, he would shoot a left-handed hook or a turnaround jump shot, both of which were lower-percentage shots for him. But Kareem began shooting the baseline Skyhook, which, to the dismay of defenders, was as accurate as his move across the key. To pull it off, Kareem faked toward the middle, either with a ball fake or a dribble in that direction, like he was about to shoot a left-handed hook, and then quickly turned baseline to launch the right-handed hook. Nothing but net!

I mostly played against Kareem when I was with the San Diego Clippers. One game at our place, in the first play of the game Magic Johnson passed Kareem the ball down low on the left side. I had it all planned out. I was going to act like I was giving him the hook across the key and then, the moment he started going that way, I was going to jump in front of him and take the charge or at least cause him to step away from the basket. My plan was to frustrate him and throw him off balance. Just as I planned, he turned toward the key and took his first dribble. I jumped in front of him. To my complete surprise, he countered by reversing with a drop step toward the basket for a dunk that had the entire backboard shaking for 10 seconds. Because I was determined not to let that happen again, for the rest of the game, Kareem didn't need to use the counter; he got his hook shot and scored 40 on me.

After my Clipper years, I was traded to the Lakers where I played against Kareem in practice. Again, I did my best to take that shot away. I had learned my lesson about not jumping in front of him. In our first scrimmage that year, Kareem received the ball, again, on the left block. He started his move across the key (left, when facing the basket from the free throw line). I played behind him, ever conscious of that lethal reverse he used before. However, I backed away a bit, planning to crowd him when he came across the key for the hook. He knew what I was doing. He turned his head to the baseline as if he were going for that reverse again. I went for the bait and moved to my right, opening up a path for Kareem to go across the key. He did and hit the bottom of the net with a beautiful (beautiful to him, but not to me) Skyhook. The rest of the year was pretty much like that. There was just no way to stop that hook, and the reason was, I was never aware of his move going the other way.

The Two-Move Set

As long as I can remember, coaches have taught: Use one primary move and one counter in case the primary is not there. I want to change that. I'm talking about creating one *set* of two moves, or a two-move set, with either one being the primary move (first move available), depending on how the defense is playing.

Like Kareem, my main shot was the hook shot, and I wanted to shoot it every time if I could. The problem was: my defender was well aware of my intentions, and when I received the basketball, he often moved over to prevent me going for that shot. As I mentioned, the conventional method taught by most coaches is to go for the primary move first and then, if stopped, reverse with the counter move. When the defender is already blocking the path for the primary move, however, that strategy will not work because the player cannot use the primary move to set up the counter. But when a player has a two-move set, and is trained to read the defender and use either move on the spot, all defensive strategies are rendered ineffective.

When a player has two primary moves, the two-move set, it opens up many possible combinations of moves. For example, when the defender overplayed my hook and I went baseline, he would move over quickly to get in my way. That is when I switched to my other primary move, the hook shot across the key.

Teach the Counter Move First

Your question was, "What moves do I teach my post player?" I have given you the example of the two moves that Kareem and I were taught. But as mentioned previously, those may not be the best moves for your player.

Paul Westphal, one of the most innovative basketball players ever, once asked me what I thought about a low-post move he made up, one custom-made for a smaller player posting up a taller one. Here's the move. On the left block, he pivoted on his right foot and faced his defender like Walton did for his jump shot. But instead of squaring all the way up to the hoop, he kept his left foot back toward the sideline and leaned away from the basket, creating space between him and the defender. It was a rather significant lean. At the same time, he lifted the ball up and showed the potential fall-away jump shot, holding the ball above his head. In this position, he was able to launch a quick jump shot should the defender stay back. He showed me that if the defender didn't close with his hand up to discourage the shot, he could get the shot off. But if the opponent came closer, the position of his feet was perfect for a quick counter across the key.

But here is how Paul used the two-move set. If, when receiving the ball at the low post, he sensed the defender was playing him closely, anticipating his turnaround move, he darted across the key for the shot there. That was Paul Westphal's set of two moves, and it worked for him.

While either move can become the primary move, one of the two moves is the one the player prefers to use. For Kareem, it was the Skyhook. Paul Westphal, at 6'4", wanted to shoot that little fall-away jump shot. The move across the key, for lack of a better term, we call the "reverse." The reverse move is used first only when, at the moment the offensive player receives the basketball, the primary (preferred) move is completely taken away. When it is not taken away, the primary option is used.

John Wooden always taught the reverse options of his offense before the other options. When I asked him why, he said:

> *"If I taught the regular plays first, my team may think the reverse plays were of secondary importance. By teaching the reverses first, I tried to get it across that they were of equal importance. In this way, I hoped I trained my teams, when they were about to start an offensive play and were reading the defense, to think of the reverse and the main play."*

He went on to say that regular plays need to be executed quickly, but not nearly as quickly as the reverses. There is only a short window when the quick score is available. That's why Coach Wooden put emphasis on the counter (reverse) plays, teaching them the first week of practice. By the way, we often started the game with a reverse play.

When you are teaching the post player, and it has already been established what his primary and reverse moves are, in the same way as Coach Wooden did, teach the reverse first. In this way, it will be foremost in the player's mind as a usable option.

Why the Skyhook Is Not Being Used Today

By now you know, I am a believer in the two-move set Kareem and I used. I go all over the world teaching this set to youngsters, but I have discovered that even when I show them it works, they are slow to adopt the set. Why? There are four possible answers:

- It is very difficult for a young person to make a major change in his game because it's embarrassing if the new method does not work right away. What he has been using is probably working to a degree. Changing to the Skyhook from the jump hook, for example, may result in a lower field goal percentage at the outset. Some players cannot handle that and default to the old method after the clinic.
- The Skyhook is "old school." High school and college players, through the years, have always emulated the current professional players. They are their heroes, and young players want to be like them. Today, few players, at least the most popular ones like LeBron James, use the running hook (jumping off one foot). So, you won't see the kids working on that in their free time. You will, however, observe many guards dribble between the legs for no reason other than to show everyone they have "skills." And you will see the post players shooting jump hooks (taking off from two feet). Thus, the Skyhook is old school, and it would take an extremely confident young person, who cares only about outcome rather than how he looks, to change what he is doing to Kareem's move.
- The Skyhook takes a lot of practice. When watching Kareem Abdul-Jabbar shoot that shot (yes, film was invented before Kareem), it may look like it was easy, but

it wasn't. Hundreds of hours of practice were spent on that very difficult weapon. At UCLA, Kareem spent hours doing the George Mikan drill. I used the hook in community college, where I first started playing basketball. For years, I shot 500 per day in the off-season. During the season, I shot 100 per day. For my career, I shot 53.7 percent (45th all-time NBA), and most of my shots were hooks. I didn't miss many because I practiced. What a concept! Young people today don't spend time by themselves working on shooting; they depend on their in-season and off-season coaches to make them practice. But it has been said, *Players are made in the driveway, not on the court.*

- The coach doesn't insist on the Skyhook. Most coaches are guards, and they really don't know how much more effective the running hook shot is. Coach Wooden was an exception. He was a guard, but he was open-minded. Kareem did have somewhat of a hook coming to UCLA, and Coach Wooden didn't see any reason to change it. It was effective, and Coach helped Kareem develop it into the weapon it became.

The blame for why the Skyhook is not being used today is not on the players; it's on the teachers. The reason it is not being used is, nobody is teaching it.

The Spall

In addition to the two-move set, there is one more move the post player needs in order to be able to use the primary move. I learned it out of necessity. As the saying goes, "Necessity is the mother of invention." I call it the "spall." Spall is one word made from two: spin and fall. I used it when my defender was pushing me from behind, with his body

Figure 8-2. Direct pressure eliminates the primary move.

or his forearm. When this happens, it is not possible for the offensive player to step across the key with the lead foot, for if he does, that 255-pounder will direct him toward the free throw line, not the middle of the key where he wants to go. It is also not possible for the offensive player to use a baseline drop step for the same reason. In other words, the straight path to the basket, either across the key or baseline, is taken away. But there is good news: The spall to the rescue. The player can spall to the baseline or across the key, depending on which side the defender is applying the most pressure.

With the post player positioned on the right side of the key (right side from the point guard's position), and assuming there is more pressure on the high side, the side away from the baseline, the post player spins baseline-side and toward the basket. His left foot is his pivot and his right foot comes completely around and steps toward the basket, so far that the player is leaning toward the hoop and out of balance. His center of gravity is severely low (about the level of the defender's hip), and his head is past, or at least even with, the defender's hip. The idea is to quickly get the head past the defender, creating a lane to the basket, and then let the rest of the body catch up.

Figure 8-3. Baseline spall move

The dribble is with the left hand, believe it or not, and the ball is dribbled one time, past the defender. When I first came up with this move, I dribbled with the right hand. It was executed so quickly and effectively, the official, who was standing close by, blew the whistle and called an offensive foul on me. The move was so good that he thought I must have hooked the defender with my left elbow, which was not true (well, maybe I did a little). To help the official with his confusion, I switched to the left hand, which was actually more effective because the dribble was more in line with the direction to the basket; the right-handed dribble was closer to the baseline.

Immediately after the dribble, I picked the ball up with both hands and gathered both feet under my shoulders, in a crouch position, still low. Now I was back on balance and ready to score the direct lay-up or the reverse should the defender be right behind me.

Figure 8-4. The spall results in an inside position.

Let's go back to when I have the ball and the defender is pushing me from behind. There is a misconception in teaching post positioning, and many coaches are guilty of teaching the wrong thing. There is a mistaken belief that the most important section of a post player's body is from the waist down, or the hips and legs. Although the hips and legs are important, the upper body is even more important, as you will see in the chapters covering how to get open and sealing. When the defender is pushing from behind, the worst thing a player can do is make contact with his backside; all that will do is increase the pressure. What the post player wants to do is use the defender's pressure against him. The harder he pushes, the more effective the spall will be because when the post player spins quickly and releases that pressure, the defender's force will cause him to move away from the basket, helping to create even more space between him and the post player. Isn't that nice of him?

What the post player should do when the pressure is applied is move the hips forward and the upper back backward to make contact with the defender (Figure 8-2). His head is now very close to the defender's head. He is leaning back so far, if the defender were to let go, the post player would fall back. But that never happens.

Now envision this. When the player spalls, his upper body, because it is leaning back, will move directly to the basket, exactly what you want. But if he is making contact with the backside (buttocks) and then spins, his head would be leaning forward or in a straight-up position. If he spins from this position, he may not be able to go toward the basket but will end up going toward the baseline and under the basket. You see, the body will go where the head goes.

As mentioned previously, the spall is a move that will make it possible for the post player to shoot his primary shot, whatever that may be. When a post player executes one or two spalls, the defender will start giving him space. When he has space, he can make his move across the key or to the baseline with the drop step. I faked the spall at times when the defender was applying pressure, and magic happened. He would always move in the direction of the fake and back up a bit. If I faked baseline, I immediately made my move across the key for the hook. Swish.

More Post Moves

With few exceptions, every player, regardless of position, should be able to score from the low post. The primary and reverse could be very different for a guard as opposed to a taller player. I was working with a 6'5" high school player who was rather thin and a deadly outside shooter. In the post, like so many other players, he was using the jump hook across the key. What happened when I customized his post moves was nothing short of miraculous.

I made his primary move a baseline step-back. With his back to the basket on the left side of the key, he made an outside pivot toward the baseline, much like Paul Westphal did. But instead of leaning back to open space, he dribbled with the left hand and jumped back toward the sideline, using his right foot to spring. This opened up a space between him and the defender, allowing him to shoot a jump shot, which he did very well.

The other component of his two-move set was the jump hook, or running hook (Skyhook) across the key. When beginning his pivot to the baseline for his primary, if he sensed the defender was moving toward him to stop the move, he immediately spalled into the key for the shot.

I added a counter to the jump shot. When he sprang back and created space, if the defender moved toward him to block the shot, he made a crossover dribble to his right and drove into the key for the easy score.

With a little practice reading the defense, he was able to score virtually at will against a defender.

May this example open up the coach's mind to the importance of, and possibilities for, custom-made two-move sets.

Key Points

- The player should choose a shot that takes advantage of his body type and abilities. Consider the set Kareem and I used. It will work for most post players, particularly the taller ones.
- The player should develop one primary move into a dominant move.
- The player should develop the two-move set.
- The player should learn the counter move first.

CHAPTER 9

How Do I Get My Post Player to Dominate the Boards?

The Driveway

One Saturday afternoon when I was a teen, my stepfather told me to sweep the driveway. He provided me with a broom and went back into the house. When I was finished, I surveyed my work and was certain the driveway was well swept and that my stepfather would be impressed upon inspection. After all, the amount of dirt I was able to extract from the concrete, now in a large pile down by the street, was substantial; I was impressed with myself for, when commencing the cleaning, I certainly didn't imagine the driveway contained that much soil. I was about to give it one more going-over, just for insurance, but like the Fonz in front of the mirror with his comb, I just could not see any way to improve on my excellent work. So I eagerly and briskly walked into the house, and boastfully told my stepfather I was finished.

As he and I approached the driveway, my eyes were fixed on his face, expecting a sudden change from non-emotion to bursting exuberance and full approval. You see, to me, that driveway was fit to be featured in *Driveways Illustrated*. But to my surprise, his countenance dropped two levels of joy when he bent down and raked his fingers over the surface. He disappointedly said, "Did you sweep at all? I don't see a lot of difference." He angrily grabbed the broom and whisked it over a small section. To my utter surprise, he dislodged dirt I thought was already history. He forcefully pushed the broom into my hands, emphatically instructed me to do the job to his standard, and stormed back into the house. When I was finished the second time, that driveway was clean, so clean you could have eaten from it, and the pile of dirt at the bottom had more than doubled. You see, my original idea of a clean driveway was not the same as that of my stepfather.

Rebounding: An Option or Assigned Responsibility?

I was a basketball player who aggressively went for the rebound every time a shot was taken, at both ends of the floor. In my day, few players possessed that insistent mentality and demeanor, and frankly, I didn't understand why. I was taught that it was my job to clean up missed shots, and I took that responsibility seriously. While I felt every missed shot was a pass to me, I saw others operating under the compromising terms, you go for the rebound "if you're in the vicinity," "most of the time," "if you feel like it," or "if the odds are good you can get the ball." For me, rebounding was a full-time, not a part-time, job. I was taught that every player on the floor has a job description, and it is the center's role to go get the ball off the boards, on the defensive end to start the fast break, and on the offensive end to put the ball in the basket where it belongs.

It's very simple: when you take your job that gravely, you end up dominating the boards and leading three leagues in rebounding (ABA, NBA, Italian) and holding all-time NBA rebound records like 18 defensive rebounds in one half. That's what I did. With the exception of Moses Malone, I don't think anyone was as consistently relentless at wrestling and battling for the loose ball as I was. And that is why I didn't understand how any player who called himself a center, knowing full well that the shot was on its way to the basket, could actually stand there uninterested and flat-footed, and acquiescently allow someone else to block him out and get that ball. To me, that was like saying, "Go ahead and shoot me" or "I'll let you have it this time, but the next one is mine." Rebounding is your job, for goodness sakes!

And the problem is still around today. Oh, every once in a while the Good Lord will raise up an aberration like Dennis Rodman, but for the most part, most big players go to the boards when the math tells them the chances for getting the rebound are pretty good. If not, it's just too much work. The thought of expending that much energy with no promise of a reward is out of the question. Trust me, that is exactly what is going through their lazy, rationalizing minds.

We see it all the time, at all levels of the game. The shot is taken, and the tallest player on the floor is blithely watching the beautiful flight of the ball when, unsuspectingly, the opponent aggressively blocks him out, and he continues to be a non-active spectator, watching that gorgeous arc of the shot, as the ball bounces off the rim to a spot he has no chance of reaching. It's as if he is saying, "Nice box-out, dude! I'll get you on the other end." And we coaches are pulling our hair out (if we have any left), knowing, if that player would have made any effort at all, he would have had a chance to make a contribution by getting the rebound.

It drives the coaches nuts, right? People go to work because they have to. Students go to class because they have to. They go to bed because they have to. Yet, rebounding seems to be optional to some. We don't get it, and we need a fix. Coaches (and I suppose parents) want to know how to morph a post player who believes rebounding is a part-time job into a wild animal who feeds on a dish of bouncing basketballs, seasoned with salty sweat.

How does that connect with me sweeping the driveway? Hang in there. This part is going to be revolutionary. When looking at the effort that's being produced, the player usually views it as satisfactory, while the coach sees the same effort as grossly unsatisfactory. The player actually believes that if he pulled down eight rebounds in a game, he did a good job, even if he knew in his heart (not in his head, mind you) he could have had 16 next to his name on the stat sheet. If asked, "Could you have obtained 16 rebounds?" he would say, "I guess so. I don't know." You, the coach, look at rebounding effort like my stepfather looked at "clean." The players do not look at it the same way; they don't know what "be a force on the glass tonight" means. To you, that phrase is accompanied by a vision of a post player going to the boards with such intense determination, at both ends of the floor, every time a shot is launched, it results in more points scored for his team, and fewer points scored for the opponent. But the teenage player is not watching the same movie.

The problem is, coaches assume that when they tell a player to "dominate the boards," the meaning of those words is clearly and completely understood by the basketball player. Nothing could be further from the truth. To the coach, "dominate" means that player is obtaining more missed shots than anyone else on the floor, he has become a force to be reckoned with, and he is causing a very serious problem for the other team, so much so that his effort is making a difference in the expected outcome of the game. Sadly, the player understands "dominate the boards" as something completely different.

When I was coaching at Christian Heritage College, I had a 6'10" player who drove me nuts because he could have been a serious force on the glass, but he never really made the effort. Repeatedly, I told him I wanted him to go after every rebound and dominate the boards. For the first 10 games of the season, nothing happened; he would get three or four rebounds, most of which fell right into his hands because of his height.

One game, he managed to pull down 10 rebounds. After the game when he saw the stat sheet, he was overjoyed, but his excitement was nothing compared to mine; I had visions of him, for the rest of the season, consuming missed shots in a feeding frenzy, starting fruitful fast breaks, and demoralizing the opponents with offensive rebound put-backs. I had happy hallucinations of us finally winning some games because I had a center who had magically morphed from a disinterested bystander into someone who gobbled up missed shots like he was starving for basketballs. But as sure as a storm is followed by silence, the next game, he reverted back to his lackadaisical ways. My instructions had no measurable positive effect.

Numbers, Not Letters

So what is the answer? How do we help players to understand what "dominating the boards" means and to make the change from part-time to full-time? How do we get them on the same page we are reading? Should we illustrate it? I attempted that at one point with a rather timid rebounder, one who would attempt to rebound when no other player was contending for it. I played him in a game of H-O-R-S-E. In this game, one player begins by taking some sort of challenging basketball shot like a reverse lay-up or three-pointer, one he thinks the other player may have difficulty with. If he makes the shot, the opponent has to duplicate it and make it, or he will receive the first letter, "H." If he makes it, the first player tries again, but if that first player misses, the opponent takes the lead and tries a shot the first player may miss. The first player to have all five letters loses.

My player began and missed. Then it was my turn. I never missed a shot, and although he did manage to match me on two or three I thought he would miss, he ended up with all the letters while I had none. I then explained, with all the humility I could, that I dominated that game. That example, as to the point as it was, had absolutely no positive effect on my player's game rebounding performance.

My friends, the answer is not in words, but rather in numbers. Yes, repetition with various rebounding drills, for an entire season, is necessary and may reap some improvement, particularly in the proper and quick execution of the fundamentals, but drills still don't communicate the concept of domination.

The Need for a Measurable Result

When coaches tell players to be dominating rebounders, the original meaning gets watered down in processing. When my stepfather told me to clean the driveway, I had an idea what "clean" was, but not nearly to the degree he had in mind. But perhaps we are making the error of assuming the coach actually knows what he means. Can the coach identify domination? Does he know where the threshold is that divides non-domination and domination? Few coaches can because they have never really given it serious thought. So how can we expect the player to know when he has arrived and can be labeled a "dominating rebounder?" If no specific and measurable objective is identified, the coach and, consequently, the player have no means of knowing when the goal has been achieved. We need a goal that is a number. Nothing else will do.

For teenagers, you have to spell things out clearly. You must use clear communication. If you don't, they will never meet the standard you have in mind because they won't know exactly what it is. Before I commenced sweeping the driveway, my stepfather should have, with me watching, swept a small portion of it (say, four square feet) the way he wanted it done and then said, "Okay. I'm going to sweep this one more time. See how much dirt the broom gets—zero. That's how I want it done."

I can understand zero. If he would have told me that, as ridiculous as I would have thought his demand was, I would have understood it. If, after I swept the driveway, he swept it again and found one speck of dirt, I did not meet his standard. If he got no dirt, I met his standard. It's as simple as that.

Players also understand "50 percent," "70 percent," or "90 percent." If the game statistics sheet shows our team shot 43 percent from the field and I, as the coach, want to improve that to 48 percent, my players will understand clearly when I tell them, "We must improve our shooting percentage 5 percent." We don't tell our students, "School begins in the morning." School begins at 8:30. They know, 8:30 means 8:30. If they arrive at school at 8:31, they are one minute late.

To improve the rebounding of your tall player (i.e., increase the number of rebounds he gets), you must set a numerical requirement. In my career, I used two methods to measure rebounding: Pat Riley's and my own. Either one will work, but the second one is more practical and applicable at the lower levels where we don't have the luxury of qualified statisticians.

Pat Riley's Rebound Effort Chart

When I played for the Lakers, Pat Riley used a Rebound Effort Chart for the centers and big forwards: Kareem Abdul-Jabbar, Kurt Rambis, Mitch Kupchak, and myself. The purpose of the chart was primarily to reveal rebound effort in the form of a percentage. He wanted a measure of the rebounds I actually went after as a percentage of all possible rebounds. The chart calculated exactly that.

The chart had columns for Possible Rebounds, Attempts, and Rebounds. If, for example, a shot was taken and I was in the area, the statistician (one was hired for each of us) put a check in the first column (Possible Rebounds). If I made a legitimate attempt to go after that miss (should it miss), I received a check in the second column (Attempts). If I actually obtained possession of the ball, a check was entered in the third column (Rebounds).

Player	Possible Rebounds	Attempts	Rebounds	Effort %	Productivity %
Abdul-Jabbar	20	15	7	75%	46.6%
Rambis	15	10	5	66.6%	50%
Nater	12	10	5	83.3%	50%
Kupchak	14	9	5	64.2%	55.5%

Effort % = Comparison between the number of possible rebounds and the number of attempts

Productivity % = Comparison between the number of attempts and the number of rebounds obtained

Figure 9-1. Pat Riley's Rebound Effort Chart

Analyzing the Chart

The numerical goal Riley presented to Kareem, Kurt, Mitch, and myself was "Effort Percentage." This is defined as the number of times the player made a legitimate effort to obtain the rebound (again, reaching to grab the ball) divided by the number of times it was possible for him to get the rebound (he was in the area and was able to get to the ball). Riley demanded that our effort percentage be 90 percent or more.

Do you think Kareem ever got to 90 percent? Maybe the kid in the movie *Airplane!* was right. But seriously, Kareem was one heck of a rebounder. If he had wanted to, he could have led the league every year. It's possible he was completely satisfied leading the league in scoring and didn't want to dominate in another category too. If that's so, I extend my appreciation. But to be fair, because on the offensive end he was shooting that Skyhook most of the time, which he rarely missed, there were fewer rebounds to be obtained. We all know how difficult it is to rebound a shot that went in.

In the locker room, before the practice that followed a game, Riley taped each player's rebounding stat sheet on each of our lockers. I usually arrived early to compare all four sheets so I could see how I fared. I was always above the 90 percent requirement.

The chart revealed something very interesting that I believe no one, including Riley, picked up on; for every two legitimate attempts at the rebound, I came up with the ball once. This was true for almost every game and every tall player, with few exceptions. But Riley encouraged us not to focus on that statistic; he wanted us to place our attention on effort percentage. He believed, when you concentrate on the process, the result will take care of itself, and he was correct. Over the course of several games, when there is an increase in effort, there should be an increase in production.

To apply Riley's method, qualified statisticians are required, and that's not easy at the high school or even college level where they are almost always volunteers. But if you are determined to give this a go, recruit people who know what a rebound is, and train them to take accurate stats. Sit with them in front of a game video and show them how to do it right. But I warn you, don't have one of the parents do it, for obvious reasons. A student will be fine as long as he is qualified and trained, and not a friend of any player. You will need one statistician for every player. Or, one statistician can account for two players if they are never in the game together. Of course, one statistician can do it alone by watching the film after the game or the next morning. And that might be a more objective method. Nevertheless, it's a lot of work.

Swen Nater's "Rebounds per Minute Played" Method

If we are after effort, there's a much easier and a completely objective measurement method. And, waiting until the next day for the results is not necessary; the stats are available at any time, even during the course of the game.

At the professional level, Riley's chart will serve its function if the coach sets the player's goal and consistently (after every game) allows the chart to monitor progress toward that goal. But the chart's accuracy is dependent on expert statisticians who have been trained to determine when a player is able to get the rebound and also if he made a legitimate effort to get the ball. There is much subjectivity here. No doubt, there were times I questioned who was keeping my stats and if fairness was applied between all four players. For the lower levels, a more objective method is needed. I discovered it myself; in fact, I invented it and used it for every game I ever played. It may be the key to my rebounding success.

Arriving early at the professional tennis match in Indian Wells, California, I took my seat. There was only one other person in the grandstands, and he was sitting across the arena. It was obvious he was very tall, as his extended arms and legs covered several seats. He appeared very familiar, and when I took a closer look I saw it was my friend, Wilt Chamberlain. I excitedly walked over and for about a half hour, we retired basketball players did a little catching up. We had met several times before, and whenever we did, the conversation always defaulted to our disgust with the lack of effort modern post players were making in the area of rebounding. We took turns griping about "The lazy big man today" and "When I played, I was getting about one rebound every two minutes. Nobody even gets close to that today."

One rebound every two minutes? What a coincidence! In my playing days, I had the identical goal. I told Wilt I gave myself that goal based on his rebounding statistics. Wilt Chamberlain is, arguably, the greatest rebounder of all time. He averaged over 20 rebounds per game. Enough said. Case closed. School's out. In my first professional season, I set that goal for myself, and it remained my standard for the remainder of my career.

Both Riley's chart and the Rebounds per Minute methods generate intrinsic motivation, a most powerful force for personal achievement and a feeling of personal success. But the latter may do so even more. Scores received from Riley's chart are less than completely reliable, as the statistics were logged by a human being who can most definitely make an error. If the player receives a 65 percent effort rating on Riley's chart, he may or may not believe it is completely accurate and his faith in the chart is reduced.

After writing what I thought was a superior essay in high school English, I received a C+. Because I then believed the grading system to be unreliable and not fair, I was less motivated when writing the next essay. Why should I bust my chops on this paper when I know I'll never get that A? The Rebounds per Minute method, on the other hand, is completely trustworthy. If I obtained four rebounds in 10 minutes of action, that's exactly what I got. It is impossible to argue with. What excuse could I possibly have? The ball never came my way? We shot 60 percent from the field while I was on the floor? It was a slower game and, therefore, fewer rebounds were available? All of those happened to me, but when they did, I just upped my effort and I was always able to get my results. After all, there were always plenty of missed shots available. When the player accepts complete responsibility for failure and success, intrinsic motivation becomes very healthy indeed.

If a player is not meeting the goal, whatever it is set at, the coach should analyze why. If the causes are in relation to fundamentals and/or a lack of practice/repetition, much can and should be done. But the coach must continue to communicate to his players that, while he, the coach, will do everything he can during practice to equip them with the foundation for effective rebounding, the responsibility for reaching the goal is that of the player and the player alone. It is his job.

That Last Rebound of the Quarter

Kermit Washington (a teammate when I was a San Diego Clipper) and I were talking about rebounding one day. He said, "You know, at the end of a quarter, if a player takes a shot and the clock moves to zero, and the shot misses, it has to count as a rebound on the stat sheet, somewhere. If nobody grabs the ball, it is logged as a team rebound, but if a player gets it, he gets credit." As I thought back, I realized Kermit did that. So I began doing it. It was hilarious to watch us both still on the court, sometimes even going out of bounds, fighting for a ball as our team was leaving the court at halftime.

Now some Debbie Downer may say, "That's not really a rebound and should not be counted in rebounds per minute played." But think about it; the very fact that Kermit and I were thinking about that last-second shot and whether it was going to miss—and it missed almost all the time—meant we were in rebounding mode. So, encourage your post player to get that last shot. It will help get him thinking "rebound."

I am in the top 10, all time, in rebounds per minute played. I led the NBA, ABA, and Italian leagues in rebounding. I still hold the record for defensive rebounds in one half, 18. Is there a connection between my concentration on rebound effort and rebounds obtained? You betcha.

Before we conclude this chapter, I need to explain and illustrate the basic maneuvers for defensive and offensive rebounding. There are three steps to effective rebounding, regardless of which end of the court we are talking about. The player should:
- Assume every shot is missed
- Get in position
- Go get the basketball

Defensive Rebounding

When on offense, the rebounder usually does not have A1 position and must work for it. On the defensive end, he usually has the inside position. I hold the all-time record for defensive rebounds in one half (18). Want to know my secret? Yes, I assumed every shot would be missed and pursued the basketball with a ferocious appetite, but

I did something else that greatly increased my numbers: I blocked out early. At the moment the ball was shot, and often before that, I stuck a forearm into my opponent's chest and pushed him back. I was taught this technique by John Wooden. It forced the offensive player to take the long way around to the ball while I took the short road.

Figure 9-2. The early block-out is a key to getting the defensive rebound.

Offensive Rebounding

On the offensive end, it's a different story; good position (where the ball is most likely to rebound) needs to be obtained, or if you will, "stolen." There are two basic maneuvers for this: fake and shoot the arm, and fake and roll.

For the fake and shoot the arm method, the player first fakes a cut away from the spot he wants. In this case, we assume the shot is taken from the opposite corner and is most likely to rebound to the other side, close to the baseline.

Figure 9-3. Player faking away from where ball will rebound

The player then shoots the inside hand (closest to the defender) past the defender's ear and directly toward the desired spot. The rest of his body follows.

Figure 9-4. Player shooting inside hand past defender's ear

For the fake and roll, again the player fakes away from the desired position, but this time, instead of shooting the hand through, he rolls (executes a spall) toward the basket. This move is effective anytime, but I used it most when the defender was putting a lot of body into me. Please note that, in order to move toward the basket when rolling, the player must lean back. If he does not, he will not go directly toward the desired spot.

Figure 9-5. Player rolling off defender's back with his back

Key Points

- Communicate clearly what "dominate the boards" means.
- Use a numerical method for evaluating effort or results.
- Monitor progress toward the goal.

CHAPTER 10

How Do I Get My Post Player to Be a Defensive Force Around the Hoop?

What you're really asking is, "How can I get the post player to protect the basket and dominate or rule the defensive paint area?" So first, let's define what "dominate" means. You will need to explain this to your post player so he knows exactly what you mean.

Merriam-Webster defines "dominate" as follows:
- *rule, control (e.g., an empire that* dominated *the world)*
- *to exert the supreme determining or guiding influence on (e.g., the ambition that has* dominated *his life)*
- *to be predominant in (e.g., sugar maples* dominate *the forest)*

Examples of *dominate* in a Sentence
> *One company has* dominated *the market for years.*
> *Our team* dominated *throughout the game.*

Dominate, dominating, or *dominance* implies some sort of control of the situation. In the context of post play, a player who is dominating the paint (three-second area) has communicated to the other players on both teams that nothing happens in that area without his approval.

On the other hand, when a post player is not dominating the defensive paint, the opposing team is allowed to do what they want in that area. The opposing players are driving to the basket, unafraid of being challenged when attempting shots. The ball is passed into the paint to cutters. Also, they are confident when they pass the ball in to their post player that he has a good chance of scoring.

We often ask, "What are the characteristics of teams that are contenders?" Basketball teams that are contenders for a title or championship have the following common characteristics:
- They have high points per possession percentages.
- They can score from the perimeter and on the inside.
- They have a sound half-court defense that forces opponents into shots they are not comfortable with—without fouling.
- They make it difficult to score around the hoop—without fouling.

This chapter primarily focuses on the fourth characteristic: making it difficult for the opponents to score around the hoop. I am going to show you how to develop the post player into team director and last line of defense. In other words, I'm going to show you how to develop something of a Bill Walton, perhaps not to that degree of excellence, but a dominant force nonetheless.

We can all agree: defense wins championships. The UCLA teams under the direction of John Wooden were great defensively. On the perimeter, it was difficult to drive to the basket; UCLA teams were drilled and skilled in shutting off driving lanes. With Bill Walton at center, opponents had a hard time scoring lay-ups or short shots; Bill was always there to challenge the shot. But he was much more than a shot blocker. Walton was, without question, the best director/communicator the game of basketball has ever seen. It was Bill's clear verbal direction that put all five players on the same page and forced opponents into shots they were not comfortable with. It was his ability to alter and block shots that made it difficult for opponents to score around the hoop.

To train the post players to control the defensive paint, we teach them to be the threatening last line of defense (shot blocker) and the director (communicator).

Step 1: Shot Blocker

Bill Russell blocked about five shots per game. That doesn't seem like a lot since in any NBA game, a team puts the ball up 75 to 85 times. But Russell's presence was always there, whether he blocked the shot, missed the block, or decided to fake the block. The very thought of his presence altered the shots of many who dared to trespass down the paint toward the Celtics' basket.

Figure 10-1. Bill Russell blocking a shot

In an interview, one opposing player was asked about the presence of Russell. He told the reporter, "When I drive to the Celtics' basket, I am well aware Russell blocks five shots per game. And since a hundred shots are taken per game, the odds that my shot is not one of them are good. But then I think, 'What if my shot is one of those five?'"

To help your post player become that kind of threat, begin by training the player to block every shot in drill situations. Later, teach him to be a little more selective. Through his career, Russell became more selective when deciding what shots to go after, but when he started playing basketball, he aggressively went after every shot.

There are two training steps needed to prepare. First, the fundamentals and the habit of going after every shot need to be developed. Second, the player must be drilled to block shots in controlled situations.

Developing Fundamentals and Habit

A fundamentally sound shot blocker has his hands about shoulder level, has good balance, and can elevate quickly. Great shot blockers like Bill Russell and Bill Walton never gathered for the jump by taking the time to bend the knees and swing the arms up. Rather, they were able to jump quickly from an upright position with the hands already about shoulder level.

To drill the quick and proper execution of jumping to block a shot, the player practices blocking imaginary lay-ups around the basket while the coach corrects errors. Even when the player has progressed to blocking shots in controlled situations and in scrimmages, this drill should be done every day. In any area of basketball, or any sport for that matter, the quick and proper execution of the fundamentals is never mastered; there is always room for improvement. In fact, without consistent perfect practice, all players will backslide toward erroneous methods. Regular practice of the proper methods will, in time, result in automaticity, a level where excellence is achieved without conscious thought of the mechanics.

Blocking the Imaginary Short Jump Shot

The player is positioned as if he is guarding a post player at the low post. In other words, he's in the key, but closer to one block than the other. On the whistle, with the feet about shoulder-width apart, every joint flexed and relaxed, and the hands about shoulder high, he sprints toward the middle of the key, elevates quickly, and blocks the imaginary jump shot, aiming it toward the free throw line area.

He blocks with the hand closest to the ball and, when blocking, keeps his elbow above the ear to avoid fouling on the follow-through. The mechanics of his block are much like that of the jump shot; the arm remains up while the wrist snaps. He then repeats the drill on the other side of the basket.

Blocking the Imaginary Lay-Up

This drill uses the same procedure as the previous drill, but the block now happens by the backboard on the other side of the key. The player's arms stay up, the block is executed with the wrist only, and the imaginary ball is directed back into the court, never out-of-bounds. The block is always executed with the hand closest to the baseline, which enables the player to block the basketball back into play. I am sick and tired of watching players swat basketballs out-of-bounds and then thump their chests like animals. That is selfish. Blocking the ball back into play reveals team spirit because that maneuver is designed to start a fast break. No one was better at this than the great Bill Walton.

Figure 10-2. Blocking the imaginary shot

Live Blocking of the Short Jump Shot and Lay-Up

This drill is the next step after imaginary blocking shots. An offensive player dribbles into the key and stops to shoot a short jump shot. The defender blocks the shot back into play, preferably toward the free throw line.

Here, quick jumping from an upright position with hands about shoulder-width is very important as the defender must learn to leave his feet after the shooter does. There is no time to gather. As he matures and gains experience, he will learn what Bill Walton did.

Years ago, after both Bill Walton and I retired, as we were walking around the San Diego Zoo, I asked him, "What is your philosophy about blocking shots?" He quickly told me:

The idea is to be there when the shot is attempted. Sometimes that means the player leaving his feet after the shooter jumps, and sometimes that means having to leave his feet early. It depends on such factors as: how quick of a jumper the player is, how soon the shot is released, and how tall the shooter is. Every player and every situation is different.

In college, Bill Walton was able to wait until the shooter left his feet. Bill was a very quick jumper and could get to the ball in time, even if the shooter was tall. But when he went up against Kareem in the pros, to get close to that Skyhook, which Kareem released very quickly, Bill had to leave the floor before Kareem did. That was no problem since, once Abdul-Jabbar took that step with the left foot to go into his Skyhook move, he never reversed.

The main point again is: the defensive post, in order to establish the key as his territory, must do something to stop every shot taken inside. When he begins his journey to become the dominant inside player, he goes after every shot, trying to block it. Then, he begins to pick his times and pick his strategy. What a wonderful, wonderful, and exciting position to play.

Controlled Practice

The next step in preparing the post player to be a shot blocker is to have him reject shots in game-like situations in controlled competitive drills. Some of those drills may be: two-on-one break, three-on-two fast break, and two-on-two half-court. The X's and O's of the drills should, if possible, be game-like. In other words, they should resemble events that occur in games.

At this stage, the post player is still trying to block every shot to develop the fundamentals and habit. The post player must make a legitimate attempt to block the ball every time it is shot, no matter how off balance or out of position he may be or how impossible it may seem to get to the basketball. This is a major step in developing habit. All the while, the coach corrects improper body position.

Scrimmage

Drills are great for teaching the fundamentals of footwork and jumping such as balanced position, feet a little wider than shoulder-width apart, back straight, and hands about shoulder level. They are also useful for beginning to develop the habit of going after the basketball. But like in any other area of the game, drills are only half of the equation for improving game performance. The other half is scrimmage.

In scrimmage, timing and jumping skills are developed through repetition. The post player must apply what he has learned in the drills to blocking shots in competitive situations. And the coach must follow up by monitoring, tracking, and providing regular feedback.

There is no need to instruct the post player to block every shot in five-on-five scrimmage. He won't do it. There will be too many situations where it is simply not possible or wise to leave the offensive post player. At the same time, the coach should refrain from telling his post player to back off and be selective; that will happen naturally, through experience, in scrimmage and games. But, when the player fails to go after a shot when it was possible to do so, the coach must certainly make mention of that.

Step 2: Defensive Director/Verbal Communicator

Without question, Bill Walton was the very best defensive communicator I have ever seen. His teammates, in college and the NBA, will attest to the fact that Bill was a great verbal defensive leader, regularly shouting valuable heads-up and instructive phrases to perimeter players in an effort to, collectively, keep the basketball away from the basket.

Since Walton communicated directives often, you might think a list of the things he said would be extensive. On the contrary, he used only seven phrases, which can be placed into four categories.

High Post/Low Post

To stop penetration of the basketball—UCLA's general defensive objective—it was important for the perimeter players to know where Bill was, since he was the last line of defense. If Bill's offensive man was positioned at the high post, he was unable to help when an opposing player drove baseline for the score. In that case, Bill yelled, "High post," signaling for the wing defenders to influence their assignments toward the middle of the floor where he was and for the middle defenders to apply more pressure.

Conversely, when at the low post, Bill yelled, "Low post," and the wing defenders tightened up their grip, while the middle defenders helped each other to form walls, eliminating middle penetration.

That was part of UCLA's defensive system under the direction of John Wooden, unlike what we are now seeing in many high school and college programs. Today, it is common for coaches to actually tell their wing players, in every situation, to force the dribbler to the baseline, allowing penetration to the basket with the hope that should the post player not be available to help, a sagging weakside defender would sprint over to stop the ball. John Wooden's philosophy was, situation by situation, the team works intelligently and verbally to stop penetration of any kind. Of course, that requires more and better teaching, not to mention trusting players to make the proper adjustments in games.

Opposite from a defensive culture where offensive players are almost invited to penetrate, UCLA worked very hard on one-on-one and two-on-two perimeter defense. It was Coach Wooden's belief that perimeter containment was the first line of defense and the priority. Penetration results in defensive distortion and open shots, not to mention more fouls called on the defensive team, particularly the center.

Screen Right/Screen Left

Bill Walton always let a teammate know when his man was setting a screen on that teammate. This communication was not limited to on-ball screens. It was also not limited to the center; every player alerted a teammate when a screen was about to be applied. I say "about to be applied" because the directive must be dispensed well before the screen takes place, giving the defender time to adjust and avoid the screen. The general rule is: give it at the moment you know it's going to happen.

Help on the Left/Help on the Right

When a perimeter teammate had a difficult one-on-one assignment, guarding a quick penetrating player, Bill would provide extra assistance. Knowing what side Bill was on enabled the player to shade slightly to the other side, not allowing penetration that way. If he were to get beat, it would not be where Walton was unable to help.

Switch

Because UCLA players were very quick and skilled in one-on-one containment, it was rarely necessary for Bill Walton to call the switch. As a general rule, the coach does not want his center switching because that creates a mismatch, not only for a one-on-one play, but for rebounding. At UCLA, when Bill switched, we considered it a team defensive failure, and we heard about it at the next practice, possibly with the phrase "Goodness gracious sakes alive," at the beginning of the sentence. So when Bill did commit himself to guard another player who, if he caught the ball, would have been a scoring threat, he only did so until his teammate could recover.

Those seven verbal directives were the only things coming out of Bill Walton's mouth. Oh, yes. There was one more. When he blocked a shot, I think I heard him say to the shooter, once in a while, something like, "Nice try. You better get back on defense because we are on a fast break!"

Key Points

- Protecting the basket is a property of all championship teams.
- Teach the fundamentals all year.
- Drill the fundamentals and the habit of going after every shot.
- Use controlled competitive game-like drills as a transition to game performance.
- In five-on-five scrimmages, allow the post player to become selective, while you monitor/coach.
- Teach seven verbal commands.

CHAPTER 11
Unstoppable Post Plays

John Wooden's UCLA teams were known for being skilled, conditioned, and unselfish. Defensively, we were a family, talking it up all the time, putting extreme pressure on the ball and the passing lanes together, and covering for each other no matter what. We played man-to-man on the strongside but we switched a lot. We zoned the weakside and were ready to help at any point. Offensively, we were a smooth-working unit, moving people and the ball very quickly and with tremendous skill. We were so far ahead of most defenses, they were still in the first half while we were already in the second.

The following plays have all been used successfully, most of them by UCLA and the rest by me when I coached college basketball. But before you call your players to meet you on the court and run one of these gems, you need to know, many coaches have tried and failed. They have failed because they didn't understand. They thought it was the X's and O's that create the scoring opportunities. What they didn't understand is: it's not so much the play, but the execution of the play, that makes it work. I have seen so many teams run the UCLA cut and nothing materializes. If we were to juxtapose a clip of one of them running the play with UCLA running the play, it would be completely clear what the difference is. One team would be sloppily going through the motions while the other would be making convincing fakes, quick and threatening basket cuts, lots of sharp passes that are on target, and individual moves that are unstoppable. At UCLA, there was no walking or jogging on the strongside and there was no floating or waiting on the weakside. Everyone was cutting, screening, receiving, passing, and moving all the time.

There are four keys to making a play work: skill, teamwork, timing, and deception. John Wooden defined skill as, "The quick and proper execution of the fundamentals." At UCLA, we were extremely good at getting open, aggressive receiving, precision passing, quick pivoting, deceptive faking, efficient dribbling, and sharp shooting. Some might think the players came into the program skilled but that wasn't the case. We were drilled every practice, for 20 or more minutes, on the basics of the game. Once we knew how to do something properly, Coach Wooden made us do it faster and faster, telling us to be quick, but not to hurry.

To run any play properly, the players must be able to cut, pivot, receive, pass, fake, dribble, and shoot quickly and properly. Most coaches do not spend enough time drilling the fundamentals, and their team's offensive performances show it. Every pass must arrive at the correct time and in the correct place or the passing and shooting windows close.

It has been said, "It's amazing what a team can accomplish when no one cares who receives the credit." This was true for the UCLA teams. It was not uncommon, in the locker room after a victory, for us to be talking about a great play we made, rather than individual statistics. Goodness gracious sakes alive, we never talked about that. To run a play successfully, every player must be concerned with one thing and one thing only—getting the highest percentage shot possible, no matter who takes it.

They say, "Timing is everything." That axiom has proven true in my life so many times, it's embarrassing. I have missed some great opportunities, by seconds. For an offensive play, timing breaks down when one player is not in the moment and is thinking about something other than the execution of the play. He may be thinking, "I haven't had a shot for a while. It's about time." He may be thinking, "Why is the ball always going to that guy?" He might even be thinking, "Someone is going to the scorer's table. Is coach taking me out?" Any distraction from the job at hand kills timing because it takes a player out of the moment. To be in the moment, a player must be thinking, "Where is the ball? When do I cut? Does it look like this is going to work or do I need to adjust? Is there a switch or double-team we can take advantage of?" All of this must be done in seconds and requires full attention and concentration.

For example, look at the guard reverse post-up play discussed later in this chapter. Normally, that play is run when the defense is trying to prevent the pass from 1 to 2. Player 3 has one thing, and one thing only, on his mind: to see how tightly 2 is covered. As soon as he senses any hint of tight coverage, 3 sprints to the free throw line area to receive the basketball from 1. If he is daydreaming and late, the play will fail because 2's defender will loosen up. The opportunity is there when the defender first applies pressure.

As 3 receives the basketball from 1, 2 is cutting backdoor to receive the backdoor pass from 3. 2 must be on his way to the basket, the top of the key extended, when 3 catches the ball. He should make his cut before the ball is in 3's hands because as soon as it's in 3's hands, his defender will drop back and prevent the successful reverse.

When I coached, we once won a game with an out-of-bounds play under our own basket. The ref handed the ball to my point guard out-of-bounds. At the same time, my cunning forward jogged over and yelled, "Wait! I'm supposed to take the ball out!" Every opposing player froze, thinking the ref would make the adjustment, but what they saw instead was my guard passing the ball to my forward, who made an uncontested lay-up for the win. It was so deceptive the person running the clock failed to turn it on.

Deception is key to execution, particularly against better teams. You scout the other teams in your league and, rest assured, they scout you. If you run a play without deception, the defense will shut you down. But, if you run a play that looks like it's going left, when, in fact, it's quickly going right, to one of your best shooters, no matter how well they scouted you, you will get that shot. Players go with their instincts and go for fakes, and there is nothing their coach can do about it.

Take a look at the play named "green," and you will see a good example. When 4 cuts over the top of 5, looking for the lob, 2's defender will take one step in that direction, or in the least, he will freeze. To the other team, the play definitely looks like it's going to the left when, in fact, the ball is quickly going down to the guard. Coach Wooden loved this play and he loved deception. And you thought he was a nice guy.

Down

This play gets the basketball to the post (5) in the middle of the key on the left side of the half-court.

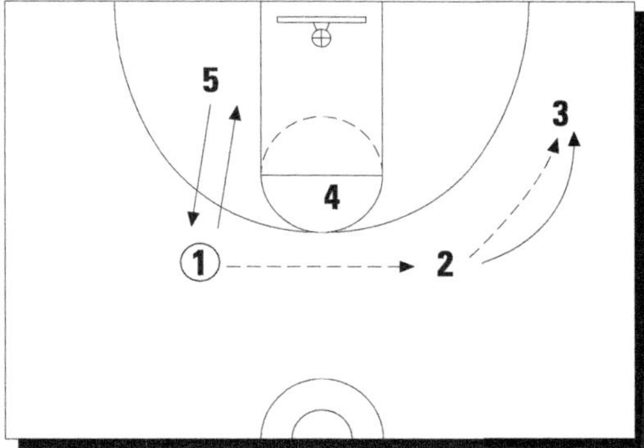

Figure 11-1

1 passes to 2, who passes to 3. 2 goes to 3 and gets a return handoff. 5 and 1 exchange positions.

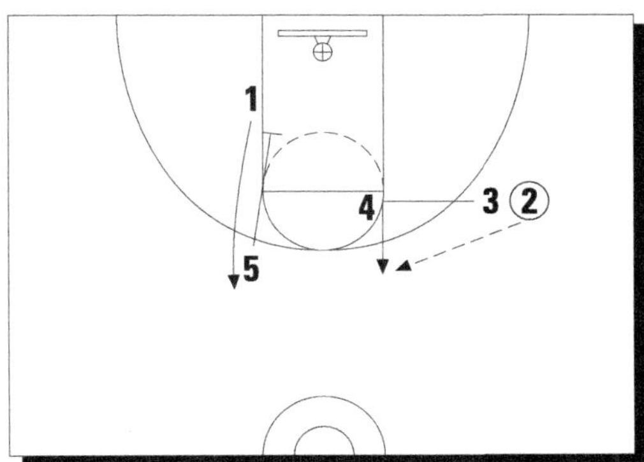

Figure 11-2

3 goes chest to chest with 4 and quickly cuts to the perimeter. (Note: If 3's defender plays on the high side, anticipating the cut, 3 can slip down the lane and get the pass from 2 for the easy score.) 2 passes to 3 on the perimeter. Meanwhile, 5 begins his down screen for 1.

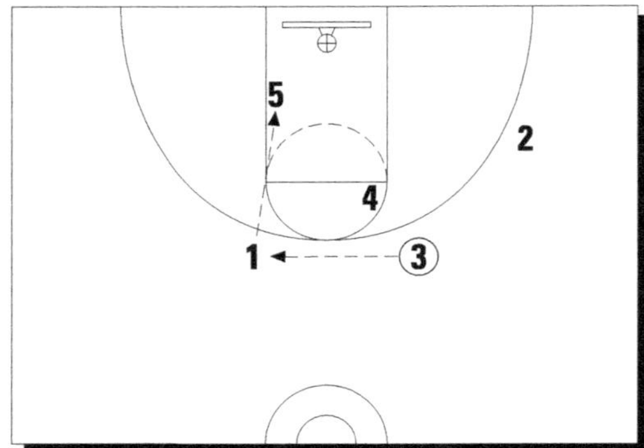

Figure 11-3

3 quickly passes to 1, who quickly passes to 5, who has sealed his man behind him in the key. 5 scores.

Duck Move Off UCLA Cut

This is probably the most well-known play from the UCLA high-post offense. In the early 1970s, we ran this for Sidney Wicks, a strong and very quick 6'8" All-American forward who could post anyone up with success, especially when receiving the basketball in the key as this play makes happen.

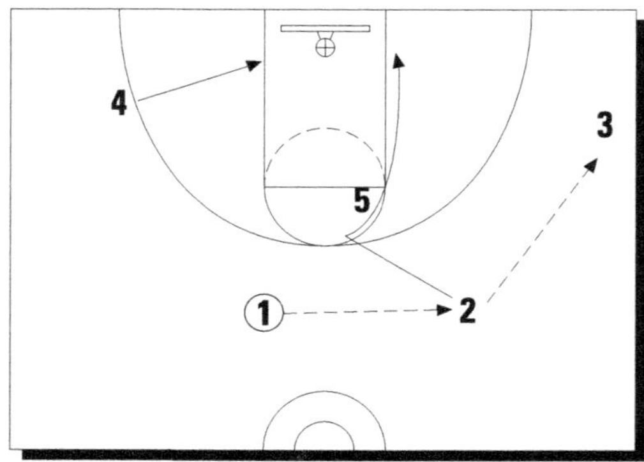

Figure 11-4

1 passes to 2, who passes to 3 on the wing. 2 makes the UCLA cut. 4 (Wicks) moves to the weakside block.

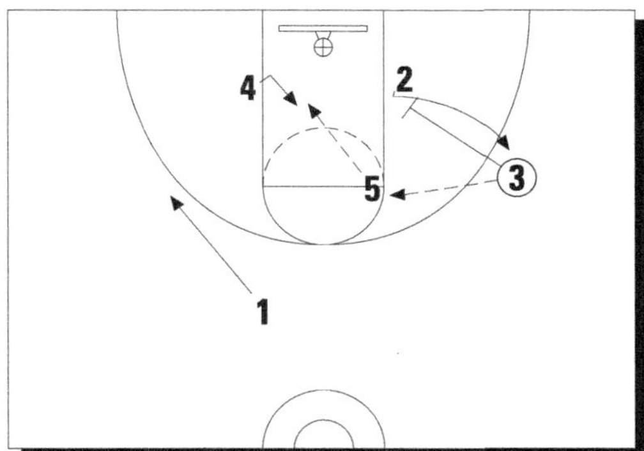

Figure 11-5

As soon as 2 cuts off 5, 5 takes a step out and receives the ball from 3. Meanwhile, 4 cuts into the key and in front of his defender to receive the basketball. 3 down screens for 2 because, like Coach Wooden always said, "The weakside makes the strongside go."

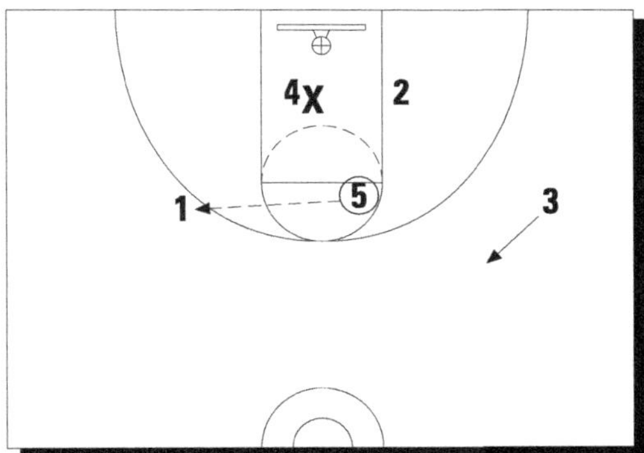

Figure 11-6

If 4 is covered, he seals. The ball is passed from 5 to 1, who has moved to the left wing area, and then in to 4 from a different angle.

Green

This is a deceptive play, as all plays should be. John Wooden created it for his 6'2" guard, John Green, who was also very strong. John averaged almost 20 points and over 6 rebounds per game his senior year (1961-62). Guard 2 will get the ball, in the post, on the right side. This play can be reversed to get the ball to the guard on the other side.

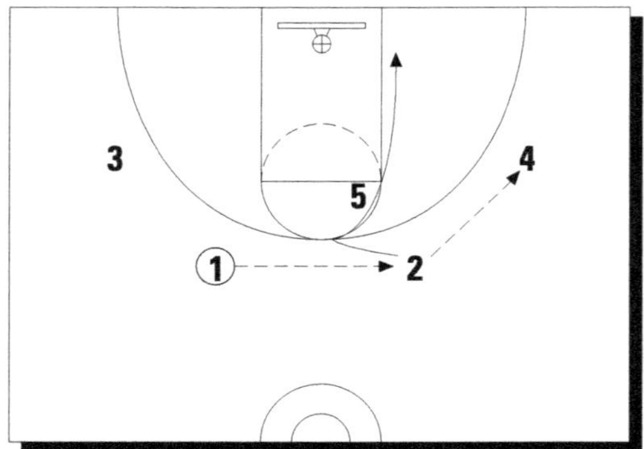

Figure 11-7

1 passes to 2, who passes to 4 on the wing. 2 (or whichever guard you want to post up) makes the UCLA cut to the block.

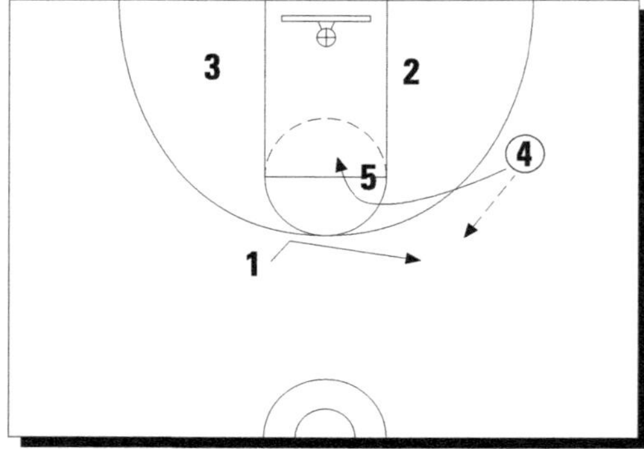

Figure 11-8

4 passes out to 1, who has moved to just outside the free throw lane extended to get a good angle for passing to 2 in the post and cuts over the top of 4. The play looks like it's going to move to the left side.

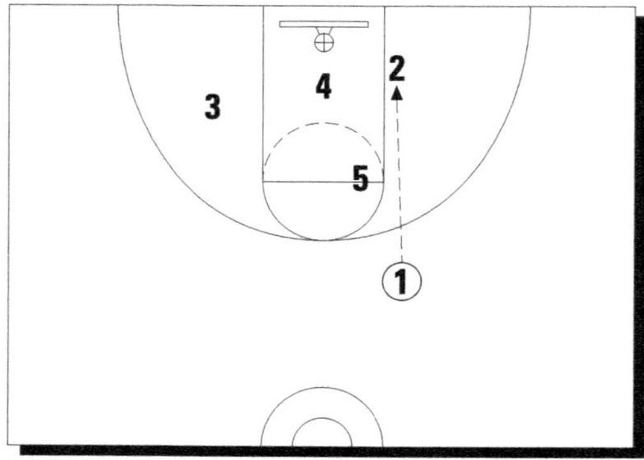

Figure 11-9

2's defender will naturally move into the lane. 2 seals his man and gets the pass from 1. Note: To sell the deception, 1 fakes the lob pass to 4.

Guard Reverse Post-Up

One of the best ways to get the ball into the low post is by having your team "pop the double stack." Popping the double stack means, with the ball on the wing, the bottom player of the stack cuts in front of his teammate (between the basketball and his teammate) and moves to the strongside elbow to create the triangle. The moment that player cuts in front of his teammate, his teammate is open.

This play is normally run when the pass from 1 to 2 (the guard-to-guard pass) is overplayed. 3 comes from the weakside wing to catch the pass in the high-post area and gives 2 the backdoor pass for the score. If 2 doesn't get the ball, he cuts off a doublescreen on the weakside for the open jump shot. We are going to take this play one step forward. Instead of shooting the jump shot, 2 will find 5 in the low post for a very good post-up situation.

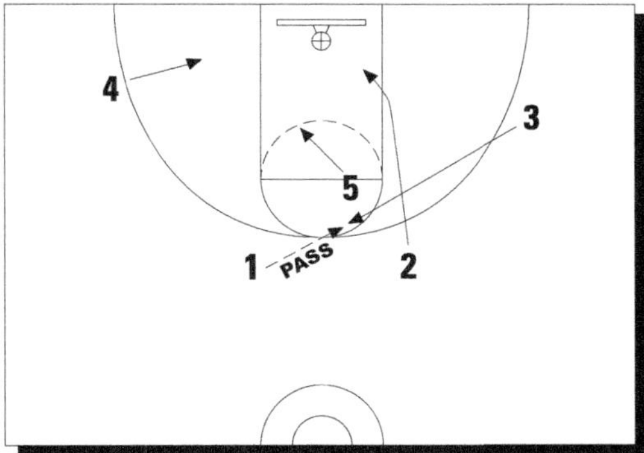

Figure 11-10

1 fakes the pass to 2 and passes to 3, who has come from the weakside to the high-post area. 2 cuts backdoor toward the basket. 5 and 4 head down toward the weakside block, in preparation for setting the double screen.

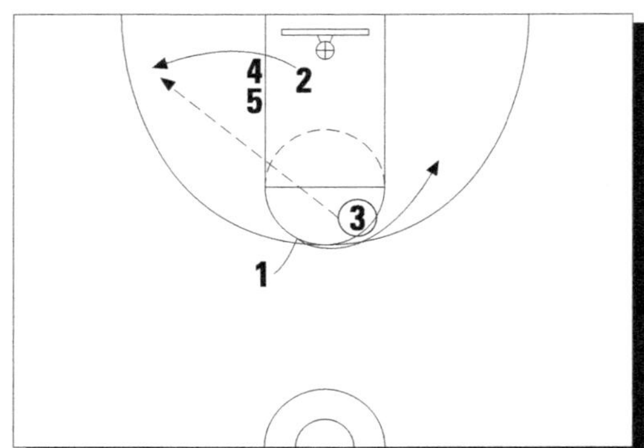

Figure 11-11

1, after passing to 3, cuts off 3 toward the wing away from the double screen. (There may be a good play here. Who knows?) 2 comes off the double screen. 3 passes to 2.

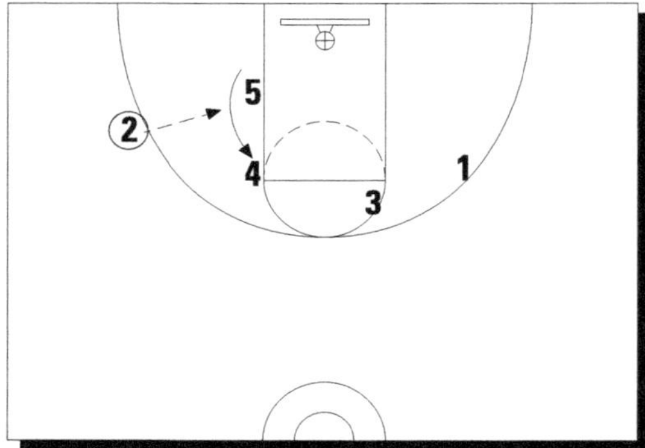

Figure 11-12

Now here is where the magic happens. While the ball is in the air, 4 cuts in front of 5 toward the high-post elbow strongside, and 2 passes to 5 immediately. 4, with his cut, opens up a clear passing lane.

Guard-to-Center Screen

The first time I saw this play was when I was with the Clippers and the Lakers ran it. It was extremely embarrassing because Kareem got a dunk. The center gets the ball in the middle of the key, wide open.

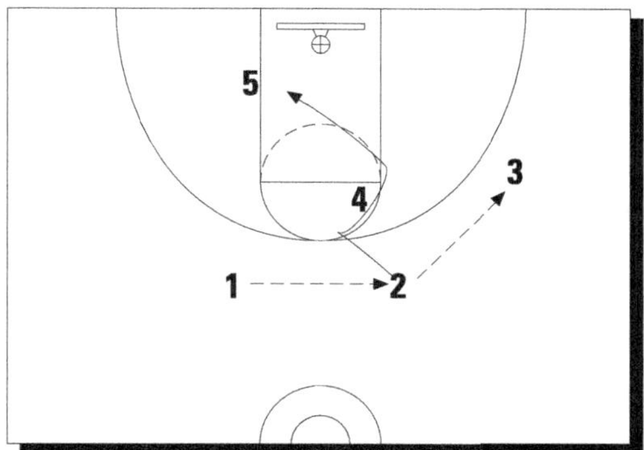

Figure 11-13

This is the UCLA cut with a twist. 1 passes to 2, who passes to 3. 2 makes the UCLA cut off 4, but instead of heading to the strongside block, he heads toward the center. (The first time you run this play, have 2 come off 5's screen and to the corner, where, when he receives the ball from 4, he can then pass in to 5.)

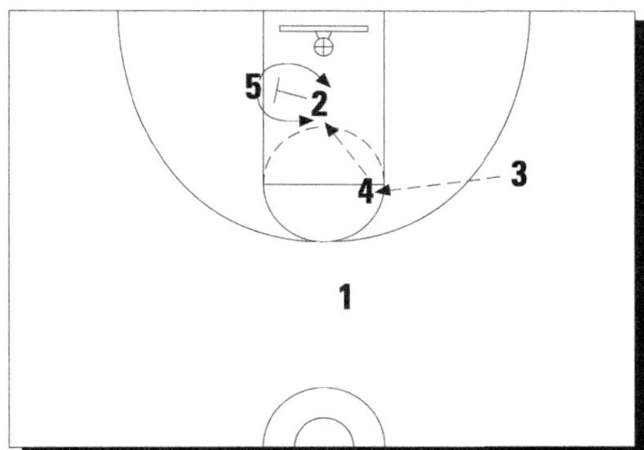

Figure 11-14

3 passes to 4 at the high post. 1 sets a screen for 5. 5, because the defender should be playing between him and the ball on the high side, spins baseline to receive the basketball under the basket for the score (or in the case of Kareem, for the slam). But, if the defender is playing low, 5 comes over the top and into the key.

This may be illegal, but it's worth a try. The NBA refs never called it.

Kentucky for Post

Deception and timing are keys to a successful play. This play offers both. After setting a high-post screen (or even before), the center slips down the lane to receive the pass from the wing player. Players 4 and 5 can be switched if you want 4 to post up rather than 5.

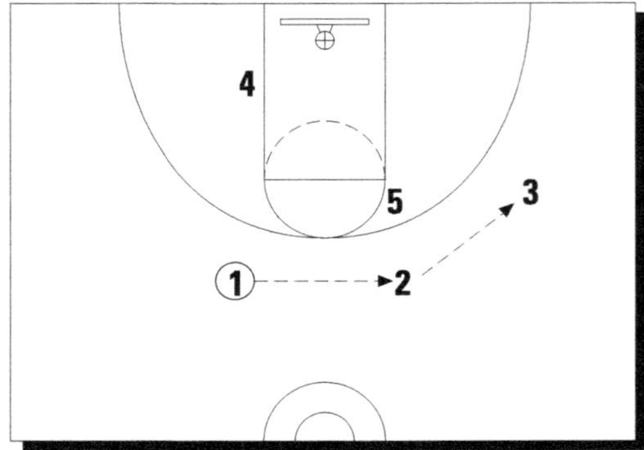

Figure 11-15

1 passes to 2, who passes to 3. 4 moves toward the weakside block.

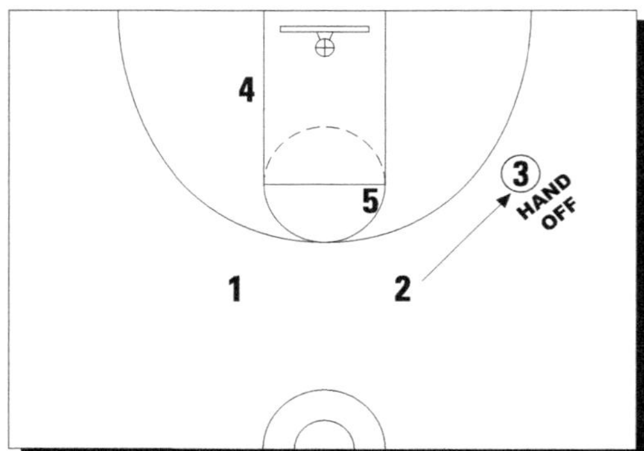

Figure 11-16

2 follows the pass and gets the handoff from 3.

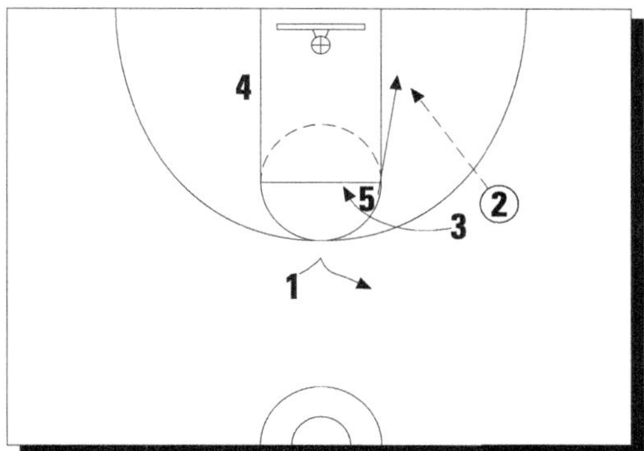

Figure 11-17

3 starts a cut over the top of the high-post screen by 5. At this point, the defense will think it's a lob play (if 3 sells it with a strong cut and 2 sells it with a fake lob pass). With defensive attention now on the weakside, when 3 is making his cut by 5, 5 slips down the lane and receives the pass from 2.

Two-Man Game Off UCLA Cut

The two-man game, or as Coach Wooden often called it, the "side-post game," is one of the most, if not *the* most, effective offensive half-court plays. With Michael Jordan, the Chicago Bulls scored hundreds of points off this play. The post man will receive the ball at the weakside elbow and the passing guard will cut off, creating a very difficult situation for the defense, especially when the new weakside has great screening action to keep those defenders busy.

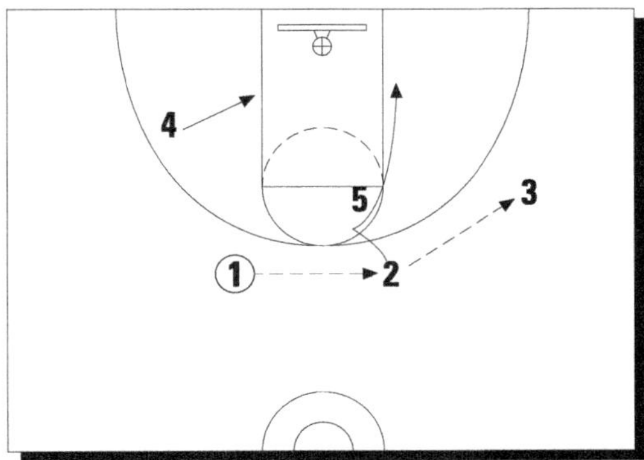

Figure 11-18

1 passes to 2, who passes to 3. 2 makes a UCLA cut off 5 to the right block. 4 moves down to the weakside block.

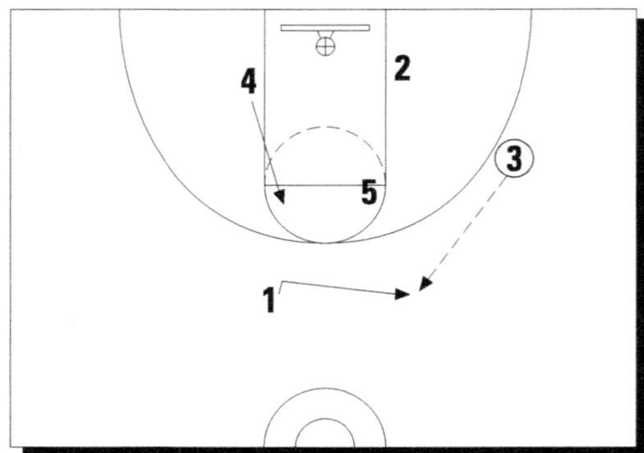

Figure 11-19

So far, this looks like the UCLA duck move, but now 3 passes out to 1, who has moved to the free throw lane extended on the strongside. He needs to be there to get a good passing angle to 4. 4 cuts quickly to the weakside elbow. He times his cut so that he arrives just after 1 receives the ball from 3.

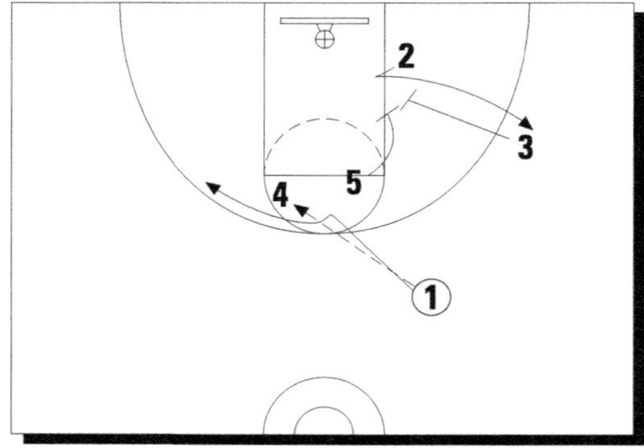

Figure 11-20

While 5 and 3 set a double down screen for 2 on the weakside, 1 passes to 4 at the elbow and cuts off him, looking for the handoff pass. Note that the double down screen should be set a second or two after 4 receives the basketball from 1. If 4 decides not to hand off to 1 because he sees a good opportunity for a three-point shot for 2 coming, that weakside action needs to be a bit behind the strongside action. But that's another play. We're talking about getting the ball to 4.

If 1 receives the handoff, he can turn the corner for the lay-up. If not, he can fan out to the wing, while 4 drops into the post, and pass the ball in. 4, when receiving the ball from 1 at the elbow, can make a one-on-one move from there. 4 can also set a ball screen for 1 and either pop for the three-pointer or roll to the basket for the direct pass or a post-up situation.

ABOUT THE AUTHOR

If someone was born in another country and never heard of basketball until he emigrated to the United States at age nine, tried out for his high school basketball team as a junior and was cut, tried out again at the community college level and made the team, only to sit the bench his entire freshman year, and sat the bench for three years at the college level, what do you think would be the odds he would make it to the NBA?

Swen Nater not only made it to the NBA, he is the only NCAA player to be selected in the first round of the NBA draft who did not start in a college game.

Although he was drafted by the NBA, Swen opted to sign with the ABA instead, where he was Rookie of the Year, led in field goal percentage and rebounding, and was a two-time All-Star.

When the ABA folded and Swen jumped to the NBA, he didn't slow down; he was just getting started. He led the league in rebounding and set an all-time rebound record of 18 defensive rebounds in one half, which still stands today. In 1976, Swen became a member of the elite 30/30 Club, one of only five players, since the ABA/NBA merger, to rack up at least 30 points and 30 rebounds in the same game. Swen is also 45th, all time, in field goal percentage for the NBA.

It will not surprise you, then, that Swen has been nominated for the Naismith Memorial Basketball Hall of Fame and has already been inducted into the Cypress College Athletics Hall of Fame.

After his playing career, Swen coached Christian Heritage College to a national championship. To give back to the game, he has written five books that relate to basketball and teaching, including *You Haven't Taught Until They Have Learned*, a study on John Wooden's teaching co-written with Ronald Gallimore; *Playing Big*, co-written with the great Pete Newell; and *John Wooden's UCLA Offense*, co-written with arguably the greatest men's college basketball coach of all time, John Wooden.

COLLECTING
AFRICAN AMERICAN ART

PARADISE
THE GIFT
GIFT OF GOD BAR

COLLECTING
AFRICAN AMERICAN ART
THE MUSEUM OF FINE ARTS, HOUSTON

John Hope Franklin and
Alvia J. Wardlaw

The Museum of Fine Arts, Houston

Distributed by Yale University Press, New Haven and London

This book commemorates the exhibition
Houston Collects: African American Art.
Generous funding for the exhibition was
provided by Fulbright & Jaworski L.L.P.,
Michael C. Linn, and Macy's Foundation.

Designed by Phenon Finley-Smiley

Printed in the United States of America

Distributed by Yale University Press,
New Haven and London
www.yalebooks.com

Library of Congress
Cataloging-in-Publication Data

Franklin, John Hope, 1915–

Collecting African American art: the Museum
of Fine Arts, Houston/John Hope Franklin and
Alvia J. Wardlaw.

p. cm.

Published to commemorate the exhibition
held at the Museum of Fine Arts, Houston,
Aug. 3–Oct. 26, 2008.
Summary: "Celebrating an important aspect
of cultural history, this book showcases the
institutional and private efforts to collect,
document, and preserve African American art
in Houston during the 20th and 21st centuries"
—Provided by publisher.

ISBN 978-0-300-15291-3 (pbk. : alk. paper)
1. African American art—Collectors and
collecting—Texas—Houston—Exhibitions.
I. Wardlaw, Alvia J. II. Museum of Fine Arts,
Houston. III. Title.

N6538.N5F73 2009
704.03'9607300747641411—dc22
2008047499

Cover illustrations: (front) Aaron Douglas,
Flight, 1930 (detail of p. 45); (back) Mequitta
Ahuja, *Parade*, 2007 (detail of p. 91)

Frontispiece: Jean Lacy, *Gift of God Bar*, 1976
(detail of p. 115)

p. vi: Jacob Lawrence, *The Brown Angel*, 1959
(detail of p. 26)

p. 10: Charles White, *Untitled*, 1959
(detail of p. 57)

p. 16: Henry Ossawa Tanner,
Flight into Egypt, 1921 (detail of p. 32)

p. 18: Lettie North, *Strip Quilt with Center
Medallion*, c. 1945 (detail of p. 29)

p. 36: Lois Mailou Jones, *Textile Design*, c. 1928
(detail of p. 47)

p. 58: Mr. Imagination, *Guitar*, 2001
(detail of p. 66)

p. 78: Lauren Kelley, *Pickin'*, 1999
(detail of p. 83)

p. 88: Thornton Dial, *Roosevelt: A Handicapped
Man Got the Cities to Move*, 1992 (detail of p. 103)

CONTENTS

RUMINATIONS OF A WOULD-BE ART COLLECTOR

John Hope Franklin

I was honored and delighted to be invited by the Museum of Fine Arts, Houston, to participate in an important gathering of various support groups of African American art.[1] Merely to think of this meeting is to recall memories of earlier visits to Houston. My early view of Houston was shaped by a vicarious, not real or tangible, visit on my part. It occurred during my final year in high school in Tulsa, Oklahoma. Our football team ended its season in 1930 without being defeated or even disturbed by the threat of defeat. Some of you can appreciate the vainglorious feeling that dominated all of us, especially the seniors, as we sent the Tulsa Hornets to the postseason game in Houston. In our smugness we awaited the news of the score by which we had defeated the football team in the postseason game. It could not possibly be true that the Tulsa Hornets not only lost to Houston, but our beloved Hornets did not make it across the Houston finish line *even once*! Seventy-eight years later, we are still seeking a way to avenge that defeat.

I was still on that search some forty years later when I went to Houston to deliver the presidential address before the Southern Historical Association. That occasion was at least pleasant when I spoke to a packed house at the Rice Hotel on the subject "The Great Confrontation: The South and the Problem of Change." From what I could see, my address was well received, even if there was no one to make comparisons between the ignominious defeat of the Booker Washington Hornets in 1930 and the presidential address of 1971. That was expecting too much, anyway. In any case, my spirits were dampened considerably because I placed my leftover libations in the trunk of the taxi to the airport, and I boarded the plane without them, which gave *more* cause, not *less*, to fret, just a bit.

Thinking back to when I was a senior in college, I had an opportunity to visit Houston for the first time. Although I was attached to a group that was studying the economic status of Negro cotton farmers, I took the time to look up a young lady who had graduated from Fisk University when I was ending my freshman year. She apologized for not inviting me to come to their suburban house for a weekend visit. The oil wells in their backyard made such a noise that she feared that they would interfere with my rest. When I told my father about the oil wells, his only comment was that he was certain that they would be music to his ears and rather than keeping him awake, would lull him to sleep!

I suppose that was my last appearance in Houston, and I would not return until I received the royal reception when I was on the tour two years ago touting my autobiography, *Mirror to America*, for which I continue to be grateful for the warm reception and the high praise I received both at Texas Southern University and the audiences that received me at the various other venues of my talks about the book.

So I returned to Houston, not to deliver a presidential address or to promote a book. Instead, I wanted to share some of my experiences as an art aficionado who, on occasion, musters sufficient courage— nerve or gall would more accurately describe my effort— to enter the field of art appreciation and become a sometime collector in a field about which I know so little.

My love for art has been lifelong, but my first attempt to translate my interest as a bystander into an active participant in collecting art crept on me before I knew what was happening. On my first trip to India in 1957, I found myself being almost overwhelmed by the beauty of the combination of colors, the shape of some of the works of art, and the obviously striking impact of the shapes and colors of some of the pieces. I had seen and admired these same qualities, even when I was in high school, but that was all, and in the past I could walk away from them and forget them. On this occasion at an art exhibit just outside Madras, I found myself unable to walk away from a certain piece of art: Its composition, the range of colors, and the clear, if inaudible message it conveyed regarding its *own beauty* as well as the vision of beauty the work conveyed to me. It was an occasion, perhaps the first, when I had the impulse to acquire a work of art if I could possibly afford the price, perhaps even if I could *not* afford it. I knew that a combination of experience and a burning impulse pushed me to acquire the work. It was the satisfaction of going through the work and admiring every detail: its colors, bright and vivid; its composition: the primitive but well-constructed tepee; the women going about their daily tasks; and the city of Madras in the distance, all on a small canvas of remarkable brilliance and detail. I *had* to have it, and when I returned to the United States it was securely packed and transported home with my other belongings. It was a wonderful feeling of satisfaction as I could boast (to myself only!) that I had become an art collector. But, the collection could not be of Indian art, although I would become a regular visitor to India as an advisor to the American Studies Research Center in Hyderabad and would serve two four-year terms on the Board of Foreign Scholarships, commonly known as the Fulbright Board. I needed an arena with which I could be familiar and where there was a chance to acquire African American art, not Indian art, on a regular basis.

The more I traveled both at home and abroad, the more I thought of collecting art. It was not my visits to art museums in the United States. They were all so possible. They did not challenge or force me to think about feasible, possible realities. Somehow, they compelled me to think about the reasonable aspects of art, whether on canvas, plasterboard, oil, watercolor, or whatever. The longer I thought about an object of art, the more I thought of it in terms of its acquisition—*by me*!

In the late summer of 1960 I accepted an invitation to visit Nigeria to study the condition of higher education in Nigeria. Even more than a half-century later I continue to believe that the Department of State was embarrassed that the official delegation sent to represent the United States to the independence of this large, wealthy, all-black country was an all-white delegation. I did not realize that at the same time that I was there looking into various aspects of higher education for the United States, Nigeria would be celebrating its independence, and that the countries of the world, including the United States, would have delegations in Lagos to celebrate the achievement of independence by Nigeria, a large, precocious, rich country in West Africa. Small wonder that when the chair of the American delegation, Nelson Rockefeller, whom I knew, urged me to join the American delegation whenever I wished, I demurred. Small wonder that I kept as clear as possible of the American delegation. I had no intention of relieving the delegation of the deserved embarrassment of not having at least one African American on the official American delegation to the independence of the richest and most advanced country in West Africa!

One day in Lagos, Nigeria's capital, I went for a walk. I went by an artist's studio and paused to view the sculpture that was in the display window. My eyes were drawn to a remarkably well-sculpted woman, austere in appearance and yet most attractive. There was a certain modesty about her, perhaps because she held her hands straight down, close to her sides. I tried to persuade myself that I should make no inquiries, that I should suppress any desire to acquire the work. Nevertheless, several days later, I not only went again to view the sculpture, but entered the studio to talk with the artist. Felix Idabour welcomed me. The piece that had claimed my attention was called *Benin Woman*—carved from mahogany; it was already several years old, and the sculptor was reluctant to part with it. He would let me have it, at a reasonable price only on my promise that when he had a show in the United States, he would ask my permission to borrow it for display. I immediately acceded to that reasonable condition. Consequently, when I left Nigeria a few days later, *Benin Woman* also left Nigeria. Today she stands atop the mantle in my living room in Durham, North Carolina.

It was my role as a student of history that provided me with some familiarity with pieces of art that otherwise might not have come to my attention. As an editor of an African American biographical and autobiographical series at the University of Chicago Press, I was busy for some fifteen or more years seeking illustrations for the series. That is how I discovered that his son in Paris held numerous works by Henry O. Tanner. Indeed, in my search for artwork for some of the works in the series, I became acquainted with Tanner's works that were close to the materials on which I was working.

After I joined the faculty of the University of Chicago in 1964, I established a series at the University of Chicago Press called Negro American Biographies and Autobiographies. One of the first volumes was a biography of Henry O. Tanner, the great African American artist, by Marcia M. Mathews. Through Tanner's New York agent, Erwin S. Barrie, at the Grand Central Art Galleries, I discovered an example of Tanner's art with whom art aficionados were not very familiar. Barrie informed me that Tanner's son, an engineer in Paris, was retiring and moving to smaller quarters. Consequently he must divest himself of most of his father's paintings. He would ship them to Barrie at the Grand Central Galleries, and Barrie would have complete control of their disposition. He promised to give me first choice if I cared to acquire any pieces. When they arrived, I went immediately to the Gallery to see the paintings and to purchase one or two pieces. The collection was grand, with more pieces from the younger Tanner than had been available from the artist in his later, more mature years.

I was living in New York and rushed to the Gallery as soon as Barrie notified me that the Tanner works had arrived. I went into Manhattan and visited what had been designated as the Barrie Collection of Tanner's works. My first reaction was to fret that I did not have sufficient funds to do justice to my acquisitive impulses. Some pieces were out of my financial reach. Even so,

I was able to purchase two pieces. They were North African scenes, done by Tanner en route from the Holy Land, as people designated the Near East in those days. The pieces, both oil on wood, had been executed in 1907, when Tanner was returning from the Holy Land. One was designated *The Old Fort* and was a painting of an ancient building in the city of Tangier. The other was *Gate to the City*, a remarkable likeness of ancient city gates that had survived to the early nineteenth century. When I was visiting in the Vice President's home in 1994, I was struck by the similarity of a painting there and my *Gate to the City*. I told Vice President Al Gore of the similarity between my painting and the one that adorned the Vice President's wall. The Vice President indicated that the painting was a Tanner and that they had borrowed it from the National Gallery in Washington, D.C., to hang in the Vice President's home during his tenure as Vice President. The Tanner painting seemed more valuable than ever once I had learned of its provenance.

On one of his visits home while he was living and working in Senegal, our son saw that my pieces of art were becoming a collection. He made that observation and volunteered to contribute to it. Thus, whenever we visited him and whenever he returned to the United States, as he frequently did, he would contribute to the collection that had gradually become a family collection. In it

were paintings by one of his close Senegalese friends, Souleyman Keita. There are landscapes, seascapes, and urban and rural scenes. They reflect a versatility hardly matched by any serious artist today. I consider myself very fortunate to be among those who can daily appreciate the artistic achievements of a person who is partly self-taught and is the beneficiary of so much talent and training that he stands at the top of one country's gift to the world.

When I was selling *The Chicago Defender*, on the streets of Tulsa in the late 1920s, one of the things I looked forward to each week was reading the column written by Bessye Bearden telling all about the social scene in Chicago, New York, and other would-be black social and financial capitals of the country. Little did I know that her son would stand at the top of the artistic world a few years later. The transition from Bessye Bearden to Romare Bearden was so smooth and unobtrusive that it was some years before I knew the connection and even a longer period before I appreciated the remarkable artistic talents of the son. He was not a painter but a designer and painter and a gifted collagist as well. Having so gifted a mother must have had something to do not only with the speed with which he reached the top but also the originality of his work and the integrity of his achievements.

I knew and admired his work for many years and longed for the day when a collage by Romare

Bearden would be somewhere in my home. It would be a while, I said to myself, and I was right. Some years ago I was in the office studio of a Cleveland artist. It was the morning after I had delivered a lecture to a group associated with Case Western Reserve University. I was very much interested in a portrait of two young girls, the daughters of the artist-shopkeeper whose work I admired. There was also a work by Romare Bearden called *Mecklenburg Evening*. The work by the studio artist-manager titled *Handle with Care* was a moving, colorful, highly sensitive painting of his two young daughters. I was very much interested in the portrait of the two girls, and although the artist had them prominently displayed, it soon became quite clear that the artist had no intention of parting with the portrait of his daughters any time soon. I began to manifest a great interest in the Bearden collage, but I was unable to conclude that I should purchase it. It was far beyond my budget. The artist-proprietor seemed disappointed that I was about to leave without making a purchase of any kind. Then he made me an offer I could not resist. When I expressed a deep interest in *Mecklenburg Evening*, but could not afford it, he suggested that I take it home, hang it where I would hang it as if I had already purchased it, and postpone any decision about it until later. Thanks to the visitors who grace my home with their presence, the word soon got around that I had a Bearden on display in my home. As

people inquired that "yes," I have a Bearden, not a powerful one, but one that adequately displayed his talents.

A week or two later the artist and art keeper called me and said that he was compelled by the Bearden estate to call in all works by him. Bearden had just passed away, in 1988, and the estate was having all Bearden works called in for reappraisal. I explained to him that the recall did not affect me, since I had decided to purchase *Mecklenburg Evening* and would be sending the check for the full amount forthwith. All that I needed was an emergency of some sort that would force me to reach a decision on the purchase. I did not require Bearden's death to force me to purchase *Mecklenburg Evening* but that was as good a weapon as any to force me to purchase the work of a master. I have become comfortable with *Mecklenburg Evening* and I would have refused to part with it, whatever the cost. Fortunately, the estate seemed pleased to permit me to keep it, and I was more than pleased to have it!

I met Aaron Douglas in 1931, when I was a freshman at Fisk University, which was hosting him while he completed the murals at the new Fisk Library. Because of my age and the fact that Douglas was the very personification of the Harlem Renaissance, I was in absolute awe of him. I got to know Douglas better when I joined the faculty in 1936–37 before returning to Harvard to complete the work for the doctorate in history. Subsequent to having become warmly acquainted with Douglas, he treated me as his equal as we were, indeed, colleagues, senior and junior, I felt that I could regard myself as his equal, although he was of another generation. I addressed him as "Doug" and he called me by my first name. One day, years after I had graduated, completed the doctorate, and had taught for years, I was visiting Fisk and looked for Doug. I found him in his studio busily engaged in finishing a portrait of a young boy perhaps fourteen years of age. The boy was seated on a chair, looking as innocent as he could, but if one took the time he could see a denial on his countenance that showed how desperately he was arguing his innocence and how successful he was in establishing his innocence. It was a marvelous indication that he had exonerated himself as completely innocent.

My reaction was summed up in the great pleasure I had in regarding Aaron Douglas as my official artist. When I told him that I *had* to have *Boy with Cap*, he happily agreed that I could have it!

If I needed to demonstrate that Aaron Douglas was my official artist, I did so by telling him that I wanted him to paint something for me in the style and spirit of the Harlem Renaissance that was his trademark but on which he no longer focused. He readily agreed, and within the year he had completed *Inspiration*, a bold,

even exciting painting of a man in outer space surrounded by various objects in the universe. The sole human object stood boldly as if to defy the universe. He said that he had me in mind when he painted the man. I was moved beyond words. I could merely thank him.

Aaron Douglas by that time was, if I could be so bold as to designate him as such, the official artist, and if I could bring myself to be so presumptuous, he was *my* official artist. How else could I obtain from him, over the years, a body of artistic triumphs that gave me a sense of involvement in the artistic scene like few others could boast? Over the next few years I acquired several other Douglas masterpieces. They included three abstracts. He also saw to it that in my collection there would be an adequate showing of his representational art, such as *Still Life*, a modest vase of flowers; and *Bridge Over the Arno River*, a marvelous, colorful painting of the Piazza Michaelangelo, which has served as a wonderful reminder of Florence, my favorite city in all of Europe.

No artist, European or American, abstract or representational, can seize and hold my attention the way that Jacob Lawrence can and does. The sense of history that he displays in the various series dedicated to the movements and activities of human beings, in landmarks, in human history,

indicate a commitment to the historical process
unlike most other persons dedicated to the study
of human movements. I was most fortunate to
meet Lawrence during his Seattle days when
he had settled down to organize what he had
done in earlier decades. Few artists could match
Lawrence in his sense of history or his appreciation
of class struggles.

I learned almost in passing that Lawrence had
an agent in New York who had some of his finest
work. I thought it no harm to visit the gallery
of Terry Dintenfass and see what she had. One of
the pieces she had and one to which I took a
fancy is from what Lawrence called the Builders
Series. It was a wide-ranging exploration of man's
activities in his quest to create an advanced civi-
lization. Ms. Dintenfass had one of the most
striking examples of the Builders Series in his
rendition of *The Man with the Square*. I was smitten
by that painting almost immediately. It seemed
to reflect the very best in Jacob Lawrence: the
conceptualizing, the work, its composition,
the use of colors, and raw strength displayed
by "The Man." Although the purchase would
leave me without the means to purchase some
much more urgent items, I had agreed to make
that purchase before I had decided what needed
purchases I would postpone.

Ms. Dintenfass then told me that *The Man with
the Square* was always in the company of a much
earlier Lawrence from the American Revolutionary
period, *The Defeat*. I was already in a state of
virtual bankruptcy and felt unprotected in any
case, so I purchased the second piece. Then I
learned that there were very few Jacob Lawrences
dating back to the early 1950s. I tried to convince
myself that I had purchased *The Defeat* because
I was a *shrewd art collector!* People who believe
that will believe *anything!*

When I completed my autobiography, *Mirror to
America*, I went on the usual book tour on which
an author undertakes to persuade unenthusiastic
readers of the wisdom of purchasing the latest
work off the press. I went from New York to
Honolulu with stops all over the United States.
It was in Houston that I encountered an artist
who was more than a match for me. He was
Dr. Henry Gamble, orthopedic surgeon, whose
failing eyesight made it difficult for him to
continue the practice of medicine, and who
turned to sculpting instead. Shortly after I
returned from badgering would-be purchasers
of my autobiography, I received from my new
doctor friend a marvelously sculpted example
of his work. It put my puny efforts to shame,
and it was the beginning of a friendship that

I shall always cherish, except unless another
Houstonian sends another great piece of sculpture
my way. You must be beginning to think that
an art collector of limited talent and insight will
do almost anything to acquire a work of art.
And you are probably right!

NOTE

1   The contents of this essay were first presented by the
    author in a lecture titled "Reflections on a Century
    of Change in African American Art and Life," held
    on August 1, 2008, at the Museum of Fine Arts,
    Houston. The lecture was given as the keynote
    address of the National Alliance of African and
    African American Art Support Groups Conference.

Alvia J. Wardlaw

The exhibition *Houston Collects: African American Art*, shown at the Museum of Fine Arts, Houston, from August 3 to October 26, 2008, was the result of an extended conversation that I had with the museum's director, Peter C. Marzio. As part of the preparations for the annual conference of the National Alliance of African and African American Art Support Groups, which met in Houston in August 2008 and at which John Hope Franklin delivered the keynote address, I developed an exhibition that explored the efforts of local collectors who share an interest in African American art. I believed that this exhibition would appeal to the museum's visitors from around the country and also would contribute a more accurate curatorial perspective on the holdings of private and institutional collectors in Houston. Dr. Marzio wholeheartedly supported the idea and also encouraged using *Houston Collects* to explore other prominent collecting areas in Houston, such as Texas art and Latin American art. My quest proved to be both enlightening and enriching, resulting in an exhibition filled with surprises. Because there also proved to be a demand for a publication to document the exhibition, the Museum of Fine Arts, Houston, proceeded to photograph the rich holdings of Houston collectors and sought Dr. Franklin's permission to publish his self-titled "ruminations" on collecting.

The collecting of African American art has developed in tandem with the growth of cultural institutions and private collections in the United States. The watershed exhibition *Two Centuries of Black American Art*, organized in 1976 by David C. Driskell, was the first major exhibition both to be presented in mainstream museums throughout the country and to focus on African American art. The exhibition also revealed that, not surprisingly, many of the works either were housed in museums on the

East Coast or were in the private hands of major collectors of American art. Nineteenth-century masterpieces by Bannister, Duncanson, and Tanner, for instance, had been collected by preeminent institutions such as the Metropolitan Museum of Art, the Rhode Island School of Design, and the Wadsworth Atheneum. Similarly, private collectors in the East owned family portraits by Joshua Johnson that had been handed down to them through the generations, and many prominent collectors of American art included works by Horace Pippin among their masterpieces. What was critical to learn in Driskell's exhibition was that holdings of African American art could be found additionally at previously unexamined institutions, such as historically black colleges and universities (known as HBCUs) and major black businesses. I found the same to be true in the collecting profile of Houston.

In organizing the exhibition *Houston Collects*, I was honored to have a unique opportunity to spend time with many collectors of diverse backgrounds. The common denominator is their love of art. This passion coursed through all of the conversations that I had with the men and the women who make art a part of their lives. For some, African American art is the focus of their collecting; for others, the richness of Texas art traditions or the edgy visceral quality that can often be found in contemporary art was the catalyst that fueled their collecting odyssey.

There are several major areas of interest among Houston collectors, and these areas began to become apparent as I made my way around the sprawling city to view the many rich collections. A number of collectors were interested in early crafts created by African Americans. William Hill includes in his extensive collection of Texas art a remarkable array of Texas pottery made by the talented potters Hiram and James Wilson from Seguin, Texas. Moses Adams has kept in his family thirteen beautifully crafted quilts created by his grandmother, Lettie North. Such works of art add to our understanding of the complexity of nineteenth- and early-twentieth-century southern culture.

Before mainstream museums were open to African American citizens on a regular basis, historically black colleges and universities throughout the United States served as both creative havens for artists/professors on these campuses and repositories for many works by master artists, such as John Biggers, Elizabeth Catlett, Aaron Douglas, and John T. Scott. Important works by their students were collected as well. Because art departments often lacked formal gallery spaces, artworks selected for exhibition were presented in hallway cases, thereby transforming classrooms into galleries. These university exhibitions were often accompanied by brochures and documented in photographs. This awareness of the richness of the black artistic legacy and the determination to preserve it has served America well. Further, these efforts have proven essential to the development of a full discussion of the arts in this country.

In Houston, specifically, the rich tradition of the Texas Southern University Fine Arts Department has been well documented in publications such as *Black Art in Houston: The Texas Southern University Experience* (1978) and *The Art of John Biggers: View from the Upper Room* (1995). Less known to the general Houston public are the works in private collections that come from the tradition of the arts at Fisk University in Nashville. Houston collectors Dr. Gladys Forde and Dr. and Mrs. Edward Lord include in their personal collections rare masterpieces by the Harlem Renaissance muralist Aaron Douglas. What makes the works even more interesting is their provenance. They were owned by Douglas and other Fisk luminaries, such as David Driskell, and they have come to Houston as a result of the collectors' long and rich friendships with the artists. Two major figures in the HBCU art movement were Charles White and Elizabeth Catlett, both of whom taught at Hampton University in Virginia. While a student at Hampton, John Biggers studied with both of these giants of African American art. I was stunned and deeply moved when I first saw Charles White's untitled drawing uncrated for the exhibition. I had no idea that a work of such importance was included in the collection of James and Ann Harithas; this

"discovery" became the hallmark of the many revelations that occurred throughout my amazing curatorial journey.

To appreciate the range of Catlett's sculpture exhibited together, complemented by her very strong self-portrait that echoes the strength of her own sculpture, was an affirmation of the enduring importance of this remarkable artist. Finally, the work of the late John T. Scott—who is to New Orleans culture what John Biggers is to Houston culture—was prominently featured in the exhibition. As chairman of the art department at Xavier University, Scott created a rich tradition of the visual arts that spread across Louisiana. One of Scott's last works, which was exhibited in *Houston Collects*, was added to the permanent collection of the Museum of Fine Arts, Houston, thanks to the support of private donors and the museum's African American Art Advisory Board.

The museum could not have attempted to present an accurate exhibition of African American art collections in Houston without exploring the unique contributions of African American self-taught artists. The preponderance of self-taught talent is part of what makes Houston's profile unique. Some of the most dedicated and inspired collectors in the country support these artists, who in their everyday lives might easily be mistaken for bus drivers, street people, inmates, and homemakers. Dr. Carolyn Farb, Betty Moody, Marilyn Oshman, Stephanie Smither, and Clint Willour have longed championed the importance of self-taught artists, from Bill Traylor to "The Magnificent Pretty Boy" (Henry Ray Clark). As a result, Houston is much richer for their efforts. Another great "discovery" was the painting by Walter Cotton of the reading of the Emancipation Proclamation. This Texas history painting is derived from the story told to Cotton by his grandfather, who was a child on the Stroud Plantation at the time. The painting was fully restored and returned to its original splendor by the talented conservation team at the Museum of Fine Arts, Houston.

Contemporary art and photography are two final aspects of *Houston Collects* that serve to further define the unique profile of Houston collectors. In both areas, African American artists have figured prominently in the evolution of private and public collections. Thanks to the sustained efforts of Anne Wilkes Tucker, the Gus and Lyndall Wortham Curator of Photography at the Museum of Fine Arts, Houston, the institution has built what is undoubtedly among the most extensive collections of African American photography in the country. Included in this collection are the photographs from the landmark exhibition *Songs of My People* (1990). Many of the photographs featured in *Houston Collects* were drawn from the museum's permanent collection, including works by Roy DeCarava—who was given his first retrospective at the museum—and Earlie Hudnall, Jr., who has fully documented the now quickly disappearing Fourth Ward community of Houston. In the contemporary art arena, the enthusiasm and focus of collectors such as Melanie Lawson and John Guess, Jr., Lester Marks, and Michael Page have enriched holdings in Houston with works by Mequitta Ahuja, Radcliffe Bailey, Jean-Michel Basquiat, David McGee, Julie Mehretu, Demetrius Oliver, and Robert Pruitt. The innovative vision of these collectors continues to bring to the forefront the fresh creativity of young artists. It is this sense of discovery that makes Houston such a vibrant city for the arts.

I cannot thank enough each and every lender to the exhibition. Their generosity of spirit made the exhibition possible. They not only are art collectors; they are remarkable human beings. For me, one of the pleasures of this curatorial project has been the opportunity to witness the immense joy and emotion that the collectors felt as they discovered new art and also one another for the first time. My hope is that such bonds will grow and that the collecting of African American art will reach even greater heights in Houston. I must extend special thanks to the fellow institutions that participated in this project, including The Menil Collection, Houston; the Houston Museum of

African American Culture; and the University Museum at Texas Southern University. My colleagues at these institutions were instrumental in making the exhibition and the publication a reality. Certainly a special thank-you goes to the artists themselves. Their magnificent works served to inspire collectors and to light the fire of their collective imagination. We are enriched by such vision.

The National Alliance of African and African American Art Support Groups deserves very special recognition. This organization, now in its tenth year, held its first meeting in Houston at the Museum of Fine Arts, Houston. Comprised of collectors, museum and arts professionals, museum trustees, and artists, the Alliance serves as a national model of what can be achieved collectively when supporters of art, and in this instance of African American art, come together and also when institutions present this talent. I am indebted to all of the members of the Alliance for their deep commitment to African American culture on an international level.

Finally, I must commend my dedicated and talented colleagues at the Museum of Fine Arts, Houston, whose determination, professional zeal, and imagination have served to make both the exhibition and the publication a reality. Space does not permit me to thank everyone, but I would like to acknowledge John Obsta and the registrar's staff; Michael Kennaugh and the preparations staff; Diane Lovejoy, Kem Schultz, and Phenon Finley-Smiley of the publications and graphics staff; Margaret Mims of the education staff; Andrea di Bagno and Bert Samples of the conservation staff; Marty Stein of the photographic services staff; and M'Kina Tapscott, my curatorial assistant. To them I extend a thousand thanks for adding this very important chapter to the ongoing discussion of African American culture. *Asante sana.*

H.O.Tanner

HOUSTON COLLECTS: AFRICAN AMERICAN ART

Alvia J. Wardlaw

> *The political vision that guided the Black freedom struggle from Frederick Douglass to Martin Luther King, Jr. rested with two goals—first, the dismantling of racism within the legal, economic, and social apparatus, and the granting of democratic rights to African American people; and second, the empowerment of the Black community in the context of culture, social relations, and daily life… This is our sense of culture and beauty, our music, dance, and artistic sensibility, our quest for human dignity in our relations with whites. The struggle for freedom has always been a search for authentic identity, a sense of "being for ourselves," and not for others.*
> *—Dr. Manning Marable, Columbia University, 1983*

This essay celebrates the many artistic voices that define the authentic identity of the African American experience and the historic appreciation of African American culture that has existed within the Southwest region for decades. Beginning with the first gift of African American art to the Museum of Fine Arts, Houston, in 1950, a painting by Henry Ossawa Tanner, *Flight into Egypt* (1921), and ending with twenty-first-century expressions, the more than one hundred works from Houston's private and public collections that are brought together in this publication demonstrate the depth, breadth, and commitment to preserving the extraordinarily rich legacy of African American art.

In his seminal work, *The Souls of Black Folk* (1903), the legendary scholar and social activist W.E.B. DuBois described the emotional struggle for freedom: "It is a peculiar sensation, this double-consciousness, this sense of always looking at one's self through the eyes of others, of measuring one's soul by the tape of a world that looks on in amused contempt and pity. One ever feels his twoness… two warring ideals in one dark body, whose dogged strength alone keeps it from being torn asunder."

Two equally strong traditions distinguish the early history of African American art—handcrafted objects and fine art. Pottery, quilts, handmade furniture, jewelry, and clothing became family heirlooms conveyed from one generation to the next, a means of passing along memory, history, and tradition. The identities of many of these artists have been obscured with time, but the proof of their talents remains.

On an international stage, African American artists at the turn of the twentieth century traveled to Europe, where they found the freedom to paint unencumbered by the racial prejudices that permeated American society. Robert Scott Duncanson and Henry Ossawa Tanner were both academically trained and found great recognition and success in Europe.

Horace Pippin, a self-taught artist who lost his right arm serving in World War I, created works that characterized African American daily life while paying homage to major figures in black life and religion. In New York, Romare Bearden similarly looked back to his North Carolina roots for inspiration in his work.

RICHMOND BARTHÉ, 1901–1989
Feral Benga (Benga: Dance Figure), 1935,
bronze, the Museum of Fine Arts, Houston,
museum purchase with funds provided by
the African American Art Advisory Association

ROMARE BEARDEN, 1914–1988
Before Dawn, c. 1985, mixed media on Masonite, collection of Melanie Lawson and John Guess, Jr.

Romare Bearden was born in North Carolina but moved with his family to Harlem while he was still a child. Bearden's early works express a more classic style than seen in his later works, and it was not until the 1960s that he began to create the collages for which he is so well known. *Before Dawn* refers to the small daily rituals of life in the South that Bearden records in much of his art.

A View of Asheville, North Carolina, 1850, oil on academy board, the Museum of Fine Arts, Houston, gift of the Susan Vaughan Foundation in memory of Susan Clayton McAshan

The churn illustrated here at left has a rare shape for this type of vessel. During this time period, churns normally had straight walls rather than the controlled curve, demonstrating the talent of the potter at throwing pots by hand. The Hiram and James Wilson Pottery was the first black business recorded in Texas. Organized by two former slaves who came to Texas with the plantation owner Wilson, the two brought with them pottery techniques from Edgefield, North Carolina, that became widely practiced in Texas.

Clockwise, from left to right:

H. WILSON & CO., Active 1869–84
Churn, 1872–82
Salt-glazed stoneware, William J. Hill Collection

GUADALUPE POTTERY, Active 1857–69
Churn with lid and paddle, c. 1857–69
Alkaline-glazed stoneware and wood, William J. Hill Collection

Jug, c. 1857–69
Alkaline-glazed stoneware with stone drops, William J. Hill Collection

J. S. NASH
Jar, c. 1855
Dark-glazed stoneware, William J. Hill Collection

MILLIGAN FRASER
J. S. NASH
Jar, c. 1855
Stoneware, William J. Hill Collection

Jacob Lawrence enjoyed the nightlife of Harlem, where he found vignettes of life at every turn: the movement of lively dancers, the isolation of a single figure at a bar, the color and vibrancy of people and place. The bird's-eye view of this setting at a New York tavern demonstrates the artist's desire to create his own design challenges, in this case, capturing a variety of moods within one setting. The composition draws a parallel between the community bar and a sanctuary. Both can be regarded as gathering places that offer a sense of release or comfort to the soul, through music, camaraderie, or solitude.

LETTIE NORTH, 1900–1972
Strip Quilt with Center Medallion, c. 1945, mixed textiles,
Moses Adams' Collection of Lettie North's Quilts

The grandmother of the artist and teacher Moses Adams, Lettie North was an avid quilter who grew up in Weid, Texas, a small African American community near Hallettsville in South Texas. It was her wish that her quilts be kept as heirlooms within her family. Her two daughters, Nona V. North and Era Mae North Adams, Moses Adams's mother, kept her wish, passing the beautifully crafted works to Mr. Adams. The strip and housetop quilt is a classic Southern African American quilt form, uniting purpose with simple pattern and using materials at hand that are worn with use and have gained a patina with time.

HORACE PIPPIN, 1888–1946
Marian Anderson, 1941
Oil on canvas, collection of Jim and Ann Harithas

The strength of this likeness of Marian Anderson demonstrates Horace Pippin's ability to capture an emotional presence, in this instance the iconic representation of the great operatic star whose voice and face have become part of American history. In the portrait, the fullness and richness of Anderson's voice and performance are complemented by the blue-and-white delicacy of her gown.

HORACE PIPPIN, 1888–1946
The Crucifixion, 1943, oil on canvas, The Menil Collection, Houston

HENRY OSSAWA TANNER, 1859–1937
Flight into Egypt, 1921, oil on board, the Museum of Fine Arts, Houston, gift of Mrs. Evan W. Burris

HENRY OSSAWA TANNER, 1859–1937
New Chateau, c. 1935, oil on canvas, collection of David Kensbey Frischkorn, Jr.

Henry Ossawa Tanner's depiction of the chateau shrouded in the blue-green of the countryside is painted in the artist's classic style, which earned him prominence in Europe. The lush and mysterious foliage surrounding a chateau set in the background, with figures illuminated by lamplight, yields a quiet nocturnal energy. Freed from restrictions that Tanner found at home in the United States, the artist was able to express himself with a palette of rich color and densely layered atmosphere.

UNKNOWN AMERICAN ARTIST
Child's Desk, c. 1865, wood, wire mesh, and paint, collection of Jim and Ann Harithas

This desk was created in North Carolina by a
slave for his daughter, who was learning to read.

The Return, c. 1955, woodcut, private collection

As chair of the art department at Atlanta University, Hale Woodruff created a number of images that capture the texture of Southern African American communities. This woodcut, drawn from his renderings of Beaver Slide, a black community outside of Atlanta, expresses a sharpness of design. Woodruff trained extensively in Chicago, Paris, Boston, and Mexico, where he studied Mexican mural painting with Diego Rivera. Woodruff is known also for his dedication to art education; after serving on the Atlanta University faculty for many years, he joined the art faculty at New York University.

THE BLACK INTELLIGENTSIA: HARLEM RENAISSANCE AND HBCUS

Between 1900 and 1920, hundreds of thousands of African Americans migrated from the rural South to large urban centers in the North, seeking to escape economic exploitation. The palpable excitement of this phenomenon unleashed a creative outpouring felt in every major city in the North, but New York's Harlem quickly became its epicenter. Known as the Harlem Renaissance, the movement celebrated what the great educator and philosopher Alain LeRoy Locke christened the dawn of "The New Negro." From the music of Duke Ellington and Bessie Smith to the paintings of Aaron Douglas, the sculpture of Richmond Barthé, and the poetry of Langston Hughes, artists in every medium championed African American culture and history as the wellspring from which their art flowed.

As art departments began to be organized on the campuses of Historically Black Colleges and Universities (HBCUs), the philosophy of the Harlem Renaissance—its creative energy and its sense of history—came alive on many black campuses. Aaron Douglas, who was a major figure in New York, founded the art department at Fisk University, while James Porter, at Howard University, shared the awareness of his colleague Alain LeRoy Locke and wrote the first book on African American art, *Modern Negro Art*. Similarly, at Atlanta University, Hampton University, Texas Southern University, Prairie View A&M University, and Xavier University, artists such as Hale Woodruff, Elizabeth Catlett, John Biggers, and John T. Scott taught generations of African American students about the richness of their communities and their culture through various artistic media. It was an era of firsts in every aspect of African American life, an extraordinary time, largely self-created and expressed with an unquenchable vitality.

JOHN BIGGERS, 1924–2001

The Cradle, 1950, conté crayon on paper, the Museum of Fine Arts, Houston,
25th Annual Houston Artists Exhibition, museum purchase prize, 1950

Soon after he arrived in Houston to found the art department at Texas
Southern University, then called Texas State University for Negroes,
John Biggers won the 1950 Purchase Prize from the Museum of Fine
Arts, Houston. The mother-and-child image became an icon for the
artist, and he interpreted the image, along with the maternity figure,
throughout his career. For Biggers, the art of drawing remained at the
center of his creativity. His remarkable talent for this medium enabled
him to capture with great sensitivity the richness of African culture
when he traveled to West Africa in 1957. In this drawing, Biggers
acknowledges the mother's struggle, while also inviting the viewer to
think hopeful thoughts. He achieves these effects through the soft
illumination that appears as a distant glow.

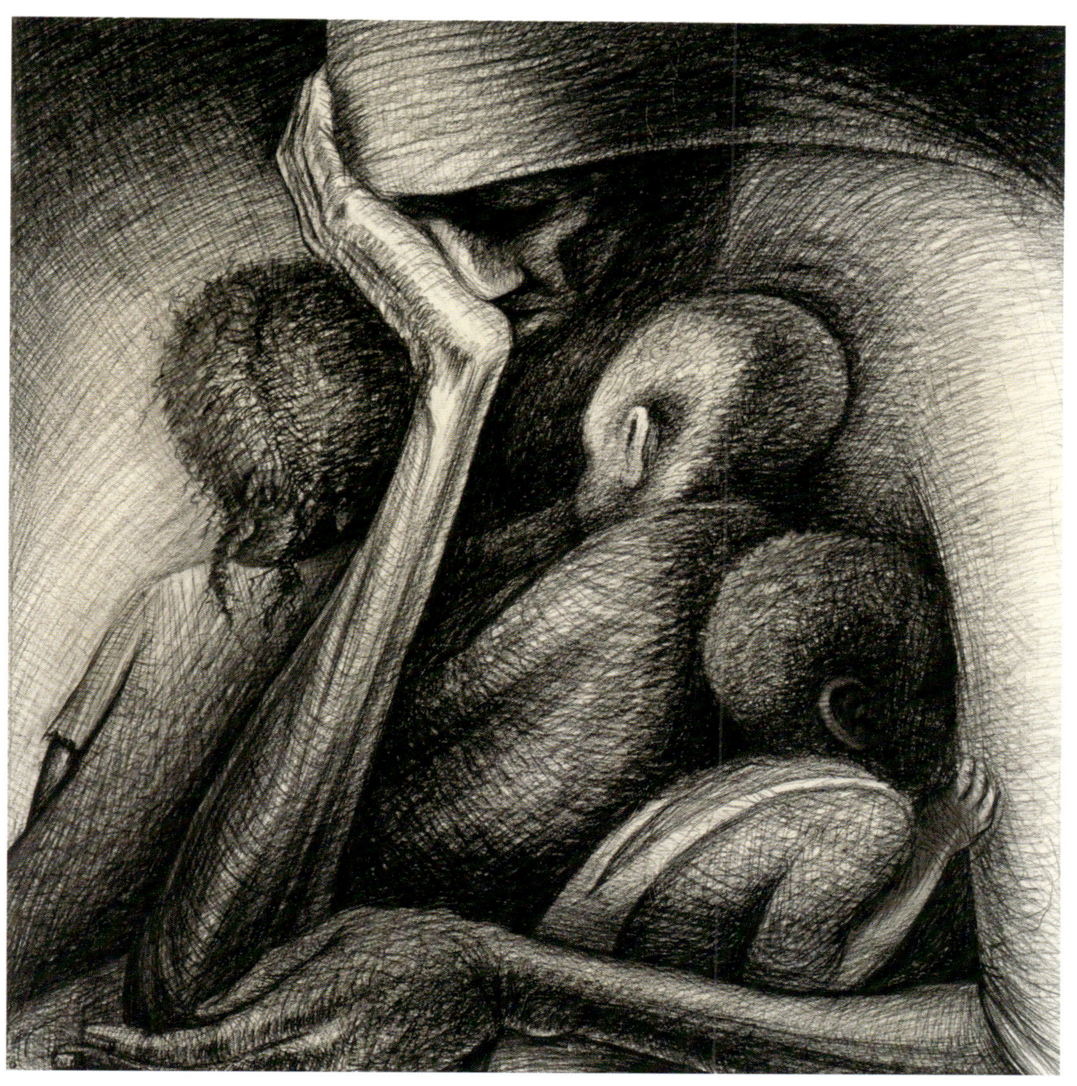

ELIZABETH CATLETT, Mexican, born United States, 1915

Torso, 1990, black onyx, collection of Gerald and Anita Smith

Now living in Cuernavaca, Mexico, Elizabeth Catlett has utilized the female form to symbolize the beauty—both spiritual and physical—of women of color. Equally talented as a printmaker, Catlett has demonstrated a strength of line and form that is a central characteristic of her work, as is the strength of her message. The artist taught at Howard University and at Dillard University.

ELIZABETH CATLETT, Mexican, born United States, 1915

Head of Man, 1943, acrylic on paper, collection of Hazel Biggers

CHARLES CRINER, Born 1945

Diva in the Pea Field, 2004, acrylic on paper, collection of Karen and Ramon Manning

HARVEY L. JOHNSON, Born 1947

Glory, Glory, Let the Circle Be Unbroken, 2000, oil on canvas, collection of Hazel Biggers

AARON DOUGLAS, 1899–1979

Portrait of Dr. Earl Lord, 1964, oil on canvas, collection of Dr. and Mrs. Edward Lord

Right: *Flight,* from the *Emperor Jones* series, 1930, woodcut, collection of Gladys I. Forde

This famous series was inspired by Eugene O'Neill's 1920 drama, *The Emperor Jones*, which is about an African American man who, after killing a person, goes to jail and later escapes to a Caribbean island. On this island he makes himself emperor, and the play is told in flashbacks as he runs through a forest to escape his former subjects who are rebelling against him. The series demonstrates the artist's keen sense of the power of the silhouette, both in stasis and in movement. Douglas is also known for his powerful murals, a tradition that he brought to Fisk University.

DAVID DRISKELL, Born 1931

Untitled, c. early 1970s, mixed media on paper, collection of Gladys I. Forde

The artist and art historian David Driskell began his academic career teaching with Aaron Douglas at Fisk University. While at Fisk, Driskell also created permanent exhibitions of the university's extensive collection of African American art. In 1976, Driskell curated the watershed exhibition *Two Centuries of Black American Art.*

LOIS MAILOU JONES, 1905–1998

Textile Design, c. 1928, tempera on paper,
the Museum of Fine Arts, Houston, museum purchase with funds provided by
the African American Art Advisory Association

An art professor at Howard University for nearly fifty years, Lois Mailou Jones studied in Europe with Pierre Bonnard and lived for many years in Haiti. Known for her mastery of many media, Jones took art students from Howard on annual trips to Europe. Elizabeth Catlett was one of Jones's most outstanding students.

JOSEPH MORAN, Born 1950

Annunciation, c. 1975, watercolor on paper, artist's frame,
private collection

EDWARD MILLS, Born 1941

True Black News, All Men are Created Equal, 1968, oil on canvas, collection of Texas Southern University

Blue Bird Short Song, 2005, watercolor on paper, private collection

Waiting for the Bus, 1976, monoprint, collection of Gladys I. Forde

Stephanie Pogue received her B.F.A. in painting from Howard University and her M.F.A. in printmaking from Cranbrook Academy of Art. As an art professor at Fisk University, Pogue taught printmaking and drawing and was gallery director for the department. The artist traveled extensively and regarded her visit to India as one of the most important experiences of her life.

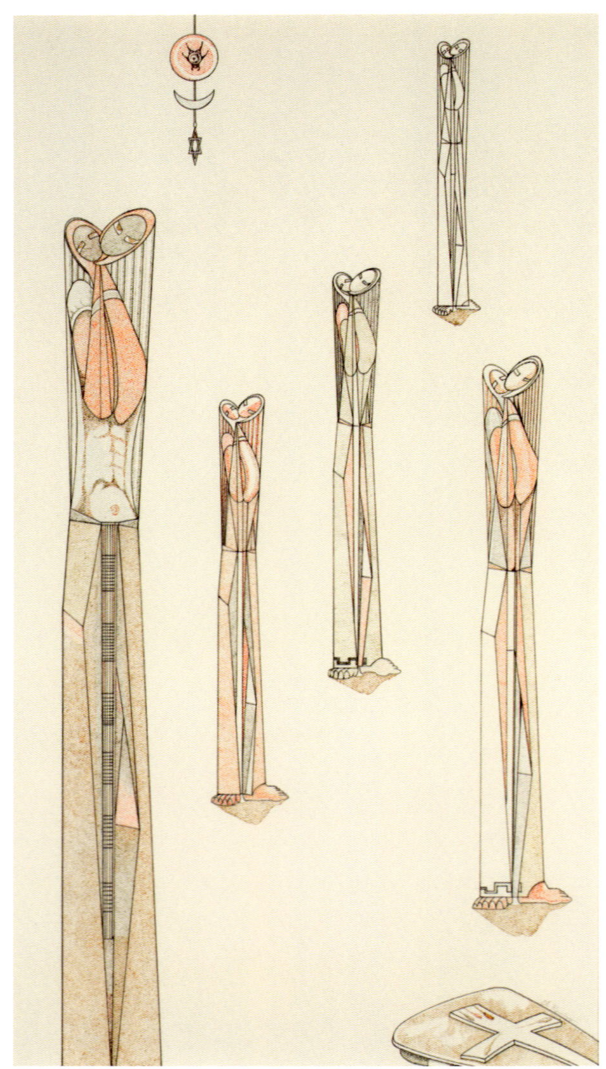

LEON RENFRO, 1937–1993

Transcendence, n.d., ink on paper board,
collection of Drs. Willie and Sarah Trotty

BERT SAMPLES, Born 1955

Her Daughters Mournfully in Gesture Dance in the Elysian Tradition, 1992, acrylic on paper,
the Museum of Fine Arts, Houston, gift of the Wilder Foundation

JOHN T. SCOTT, 1940–2007
Fats Waller, 2005, mixed media on paper, collection of Anna Rita Scott

JOHN T. SCOTT, 1940–2007
Reliquaries #4, 2000, bronze,
the Museum of Fine Arts, Houston, museum purchase with funds provided
by the African American Art Advisory Association, with additional gifts
from Annette C. Bracey, Melanie Lawson and John Guess, Jr.,
Alvia J. Wardlaw, and Hazel Biggers in memory of John T. Scott

Left:
CARROLL HARRIS SIMMS, Born 1924
Bowl, c. 1955, glazed stoneware, private collection

Right:
JESSE SIFUENTES, Born 1954
Bowl, 1972, salt-glazed stoneware,
Collection of University Museum, Texas Southern University

Jesse Sifuentes studied under Carroll Harris Simms and is now teaching ceramics in the Fine Arts Department at Texas Southern University.

Untitled, 1959, charcoal on paper, collection of Jim and Ann Harithas

Charles White's sublime mastery of line and form elevates each of his drawings to the monumental. While an art professor at Hampton University, White shared his profound talent with and made a lifelong impression on the then-young artists John Biggers and Joseph Mack. In this drawing, White depicts his subject in a posture of openness and grace. The figure acquires timelessness through the deliberate omission of a background, a technique that White used in many of his drawings.

THE URGE TO CREATE

The South has long been home to an especially rich and varied tradition of self-taught artists who have created a vast array of objects for both utilitarian and decorative purposes. These works, sometimes labeled "naïve art" or "folk art," spring from the fertile imaginations of people for whom the urge to create is totally devoid of formal training or academic rule. Rather, the urge to create expresses itself with abandon.

Houston is home to many self-taught artists, among them Henry Ray Clark, or "The Magnificent Pretty Boy," in the Third Ward; Jeff McKissack, a postal worker who spent his golden years creating the Orange Show; Cleveland Turner and his Flowercycle; and John Milkovisch and his whimsical Beer Can House. Perhaps it is no coincidence that Houston is home to the largest public display of self-taught artistic expression in the world, the annual Art Car Parade.

The Museum of Fine Arts, Houston, has organized major exhibitions of self-taught art, including two exhibitions of the quilts created by the African American women who live in the tiny community of Gee's Bend, Alabama, and the monumental constructions of Thornton Dial, Sr. The museum also has taken an active lead in collecting the work of other African American self-taught artists, including William Edmondson, Lonnie Holley, and Charles Smith.

Much self-taught art defies categorization. But the freshness of the works illustrated on the following pages reflects the willingness of Houston and its collectors both to take chances and to be on the cutting edge of the discussion about what makes art.

HENRY RAY CLARK, 1936–2006
"The Magnificent Pretty Boy," 1988, ink on manila envelope,
The Menil Collection, Houston

Like Frank Jones, Henry Ray Clark, known as "The Magnificent Pretty Boy," was repeatedly incarcerated during his lifetime. While in jail, Clark created art using manila file folders, prison requisition forms, and any other materials that were available to him.

WALTER COTTON, 1892–1978
Reading of the Emancipation Proclamation,
n.d., oil on canvas, collection of Marilyn Oshman

This painting was inspired by a story told to the artist by his grandfather, who as a child lived on the Stroud Plantation and witnessed the reading of the Emancipation Proclamation. The child shown running in front of the fence is, in fact, Cotton's grandfather. This very personal perspective of what is now known as "Juneteenth" in Texas takes the viewer back to that historic moment.

VANZANT DRIVER, Born 1957

Chapel, n.d., glass, mirror, and wood, collection of Betty Moody and Bill Steffy

Eagle, c. 1930s, limestone, the Museum of Fine Arts, Houston,
gift of Charles Tate, Mac Dunwoody, Robin Gibbs, and Lee Godfrey in honor of
James A. Elkins, Jr., at "One Great Night in November, 2005"

William Edmondson, the first African American artist to have a solo exhibition at the Museum of Modern Art, in New York, was born to former slaves and did not begin sculpting until he was sixty years old. Edmondson carved tombstones for a living and in his spare time created birds, angels, and other forms he enjoyed. It was his spareness of means that delighted early collectors of his work.

THE REVEREND JOHN L. HUNTER, 1905–1999

Acrobat with Elephants, c. 1985, wood, varnish, paint, glitter, and glass, the Museum of
Fine Arts, Houston, gift of Clinton T. Willour in honor of Betty Moody

CLEMENTINE HUNTER, 1886–1988
Baptism, n.d., acrylic on canvas board, collection of Stephanie K. Smither

MR. IMAGINATION, Born 1948
Guitar, 2001,
bottle caps, guitar, wood putty, and paint,
collection of Dr. Carolyn Farb

Born in Chicago and reared as the third of
nine children, Mr. Imagination creates bright
and beautiful works from found materials.
His signature media is the bottle cap, and he
adorns objects and figures with this simple
element. The artist became deeply interested in Egyptian art and other ancient African
cultures while creating small sculptures
made from burned sandstone that was discarded from a local foundry.

To Water You (Labor's Drawer is Empty), 1994, wood, metal bucket, and shells,
the Museum of Fine Arts, Houston, gift of Tinwood Alliance

FRANK JONES, 1900–1969
Untitled, c. 1968, colored pencil and graphite on paper, collection of Stephanie K. Smither

Known for his intricately drawn structures with "haints," or spirits, inhabiting a labyrinth of interior rooms, Frank Jones occupied his time creating art for many years while incarcerated at Huntsville State Prison in Texas. In his works, he used red and blue laundry markers for color, creating fields of pattern reminiscent of medieval manuscripts.

RONALD LOCKETT, 1965–1998
Once There Were Many, 1993, tin, nails, and graphite on wood,
the Museum of Fine Arts, Houston, museum purchase with funds provided by
the Caroline Wiess Law Accessions Endowment Fund

SISTER GERTRUDE MORGAN, 1900–1980

New Jerusalem, c. 1960, acrylic, tempera, and pen on paper, collection of Stephanie K. Smither

A street missionary in New Orleans, Sister Gertrude painted
her visions of God on everything, including window shades.
Her concept of God and Jesus was contemporary; she
depicted them in airplanes and playing Ping-Pong in heaven.

NAOMI POLK, 1892–1984

Look Down That Lonesome Road, c. 1975, crayon, watercolor, and
ink on paper with textile edging and wallpaper, mounted on cardboard,
collection of Houston Museum of African American Culture

A Houston artist and poet who lived in the Fourth Ward, Naomi
Polk began creating art in her home, painting flower pots, writing extensive poetry in thick notebooks, and creating sketches
inspired by biblical scripture. One of her favorite images was
that of the "lonesome road," her visual symbol of life's journey.

Although he lacked formal training, Dr. Charles Smith began to create a sculptural landscape in 1968 to honor the more than seven thousand African Americans who died in the Vietnam War. Now, through his art, he has developed a history of the black experience, honoring icons of the twentieth century. His sculptures often evolve over time, taking on new elements and stories from the surrounding environment.

ISAAC SMITH, Born 1944
Whale, c. 1980, wood and paint, the Museum of Fine Arts, Houston,
gift of Clinton T. Willour in honor of Stephanie Smither

BILL TRAYLOR, 1854–1949
Two Men Fighting, c. 1943, paint and pencil on paper board,
collection of Stephanie K. Smither

When he was eighty-five years old, Bill Traylor began to draw in earnest, and between 1939 and 1942 he created an estimated 1,200 to 1,500 paintings and drawings, mostly on discarded pieces of paper using tempera, graphite, and crayon. Most of these works were gathered by fellow artist Charles Shannon, who, following Traylor's death, tried to introduce the art world to Traylor's work when there was little interest in self-taught artists. Shannon kept Traylor's works safe for more than forty years, until he found galleries interested in the art in the late 1970s.

Going to Hell, 1990–91, oil on canvas, collection of Stephanie K. Smither

PURVIS YOUNG, Born 1943

Rejoice, 1991, acrylic and latex on wood and canvas, the Museum of Fine Arts, Houston, museum purchase with funds provided by the Caroline Wiess Law Accessions Endowment Fund

JOSEPH YOAKUM, 1890–1972

Gascanade River in Ozark Mountain Range at Newberg Missouri on Frisco Railroad, c. 1969–70,
colored pen and pencil on paper, collection of Stephanie K. Smither

Since its founding in 1976, the photography collection at the Museum of Fine Arts, Houston, has grown from a few hundred photographs to a world-renowned collection of more than twenty-two thousand works that span the history of photography. On the following pages is a sampling of works from the collection by African American photographers that includes Gordon Parks, the first African American photographer to work for *Life* magazine.

Photographs of the Civil Rights Movement are one of the great strengths of the collection. Dr. Martin Luther King, Jr., was highly aware of the power of the media to graphically communicate the violence and brutality endured by protesters, and he harnessed that power to turn public opinion against segregation and to build the momentum needed for social change. Ernest C. Withers's photographs are part of a larger portfolio titled *I Am A Man*, which was named for a sign carried in the Memphis sanitation workers strike in 1968. A self-taught photojournalist, Withers documented the momentous events of the Civil Rights Movement throughout the 1950s and 1960s, up through the last days of Dr. King's life. Houston-based Louise Martin photographed Dr. King's funeral for Houston's *Forward Times* and *The Informer*.

In 1990, Time Warner Inc. commissioned forty-three African American photographers, a mix of seasoned veterans and innovative young artists, to capture the African American experience. Crossing the United States in search of subjects, the photographers made more than sixty-five thousand images, from which one hundred and fifty were selected for the traveling exhibition *Songs of My People*. The works were alternatively celebrations and calls for change. At the completion of the tour, Time Warner gave the one hundred and fifty photographs in the exhibition to the Museum of Fine Arts, Houston.

EMIL CADOO, 1926–2002

James Baldwin, c. 1960, gelatin silver photograph, the Museum of Fine Arts, Houston, gift of Carol Ross

CHESTER HIGGINS, JR., Born 1946
Young Moslem Woman, Brooklyn, 1990, gelatin silver photograph,
the Museum of Fine Arts, Houston, museum purchase with funds provided by Photo Forum 1996

EARLIE HUDNALL, JR., Born 1946
Girl with Flag, 1991, gelatin silver photograph, collection of Hazel Biggers

LAUREN KELLEY, Born 1972

Pickin', 1999, chromogenic photograph, collection of Dr. and Mrs. Danny Kelley

LOUISE OZELL MARTIN , 1911–1995

Dr. King's Casket at Morehouse College, 1968, gelatin silver photograph, the Museum of Fine Arts, Houston, gift of Dr. Sarah Trotty, Joan Morgenstern, and Clinton T. Willour

Storefront Women in Harlem, 1963, gelatin silver photograph, the Museum of Fine Arts, Houston, gift of Gay Block

THE REVEREND CLARENCE TALLEY, SR., Born 1951

Sister Sister, 2002, chromogenic photograph,
collection of Drs. Willie and Sarah Trotty

ERNEST C. WITHERS, 1922–2007

I Am A Man, Sanitation Workers Strike, Memphis, Tennessee. From the portfolio *I Am A Man, Photographs by Ernest C. Withers*, Panoptican Press, 1994; March 28, 1968, gelatin silver photograph, printed 1994, edition 9/35, the Museum of Fine Arts, Houston, museum purchase with funds provided by the African American Art Advisory Association

The current generation of African American artists interprets the uniqueness of the African American experience through a global lens. Inspired by the genius and groundbreaking originality of Jean-Michel Basquiat, whose work catapulted the artist to the center of the international art world; by the incendiary deconstructions of stereotypical imagery in the fearless expressions of Michael Ray Charles; and by the work of regional artists such as Radcliffe Bailey, Jean Lacy, Annette Lawrence, David McGee, and Kermit Oliver, the newest generation has erased the boundaries that previously defined African American art. The definitive impact of technology is strongly felt in the innovative new approaches these artists bring to classic subject matter, extending the legacy of the ideas first expressed in the Harlem Renaissance into a twenty-first-century world.

A compelling number of young African American artists from Houston are establishing significant careers in the international art world. Most recently Julie Mehretu (who was a Core Artist in Residence at the Glassell School of Art at the Museum of Fine Arts, Houston), Otabenga Jones (the collaborative group composed of the artists Robert Pruitt, Jabari Anderson, Jamal Cyrus, and Kenya Evans), Trenton Doyle Hancock, and Demetrius Oliver (also a Core Artist in Residence) have captured the attention of critics and collectors with their debuts in New York at Whitney Biennials, and with securing New York museum residencies and highly successful gallery affiliations.

Since the 1990s, Houston has launched new artistic talents who have been nurtured by the availability of affordable studio space, supportive programs like the Core program at the Glassell School of Art, dedicated exhibition spaces, and enthusiastic collectors who have the confidence and the courage to collect works by artists who have not yet reached their fully mature voices.

MEQUITTA AHUJA, Born 1976

Parade, 2007, oil on canvas, collection of Melanie Lawson and John Guess, Jr.

Left:
TINA ALLEN, Born 1955
Sula, 1999, bronze, collection of Betty M. Sanders, Ph.D.

Right:
Grace, 1999, bronze, collection of Betty M. Sanders, Ph.D.

GULLAH SCI-FI MYSTERIES
Featuring
MaE
10¢
FEB.
#33
A MYSTERIOUS time traveler from the past!
Try 100 years from the PAST!
The trial of
MADAM-ETHIOPIA

DAWOLU JABARI ANDERSON, Born 1973
Madame Ethiopia, 2007, acrylic and paint marker on paper,
collection of Bill and Stephanie Perkins

A member of the artists' collective Otabenga Jones and Associates, Dawolu Jabari Anderson has long been interested in the interpretation of black history in vehicles of popular culture such as comic books. Anderson's large-scale works on paper, which combine figures drawn in the dramatic and highly stylized manner of comic strips, employ his own biting wordplay. In this drawing, the artist explores the concept of the superheroine, taking her back to her Ethiopian roots, while paying tribute to the artist John Biggers with a visual reference to his *Shotguns Third Ward*.

RADCLIFFE BAILEY, Born 1968

Grace, 1995, mixed media and found objects, collection of Lester Marks

Adam in Distress, 2007, black-and-white Prisma color on brown paper over Masonite, collection of Michael W. Page

JEAN-MICHEL BASQUIAT, 1960–1988

2. Recling Nude, 1983, oil stick on paper, collection of Lester Marks

Born in New York City of Puerto Rican and Haitian ancestry, Jean-Michel Basquiat demonstrated from an early age his exceptional talent for art. Encouraged by his mother to draw and paint, Basquiat had several breakthrough solo exhibitions in the early 1980s, leading to his inclusion in the 1983 Whitney Biennial. Befriended by Andy Warhol during this decade, the two artists created several collaborative works. This work demonstrates Basquiat's mastery of drawing the human form. He draws the reclining nude with a raw energy, yielding a figure that, although in repose, has a dynamic presence.

Antelope, 1991, wood, collection of Drs. Willie and Sarah Trotty

LIBERTY BROS.
PERMANENT-DAILY
CIRCUS
AN
ARMY
OF CLOWNS
THE GREATEST SHOW ON EARTH
MICHAEL RAY CHARLES 95
DISTRIBUTED BY LIBERTY-PERM PRODUCTS, INC.

Michael Ray Charles combines his studies in advertising and design with his preferred medium of painting as he investigates stereotypes drawn from the history of American advertising, product packaging, billboards, and commercials. In his work, the artist has turned the notion of stereotyping on its head and thrusts such images back in the face of the viewer, with a deliberate spin toward the edge.

Roosevelt: A Handicapped Man Got the Cities to Move, 1992, enamel and mixed media on wood, the Museum of Fine Arts, Houston, museum purchase with funds provided by the Caroline Wiess Law Accessions Endowment Fund

Although he has been described as self-taught, Thornton Dial is an artist who defies categorization. In his paintings, drawings, and assemblages, the artist expresses a sensibility and perspective that is entirely contemporary. Dial worked for many years as a welder, constructing Pullman railroad cars at a plant in Bessemer, Alabama. The physicality of this work is at the heart of his creativity. Dial pays homage to President Franklin D. Roosevelt and his visionary leadership in the development of the New Deal. Two tigers that move sleekly through the composition symbolize the president's display of strength and progressiveness, despite the challenges he faced living with a physical disability.

BURFORD EVANS, Born 1931

Portrait of Dr. Herman Mabrie, III, 2002, acrylic on canvas, collection of Dr. Herman Mabrie, III

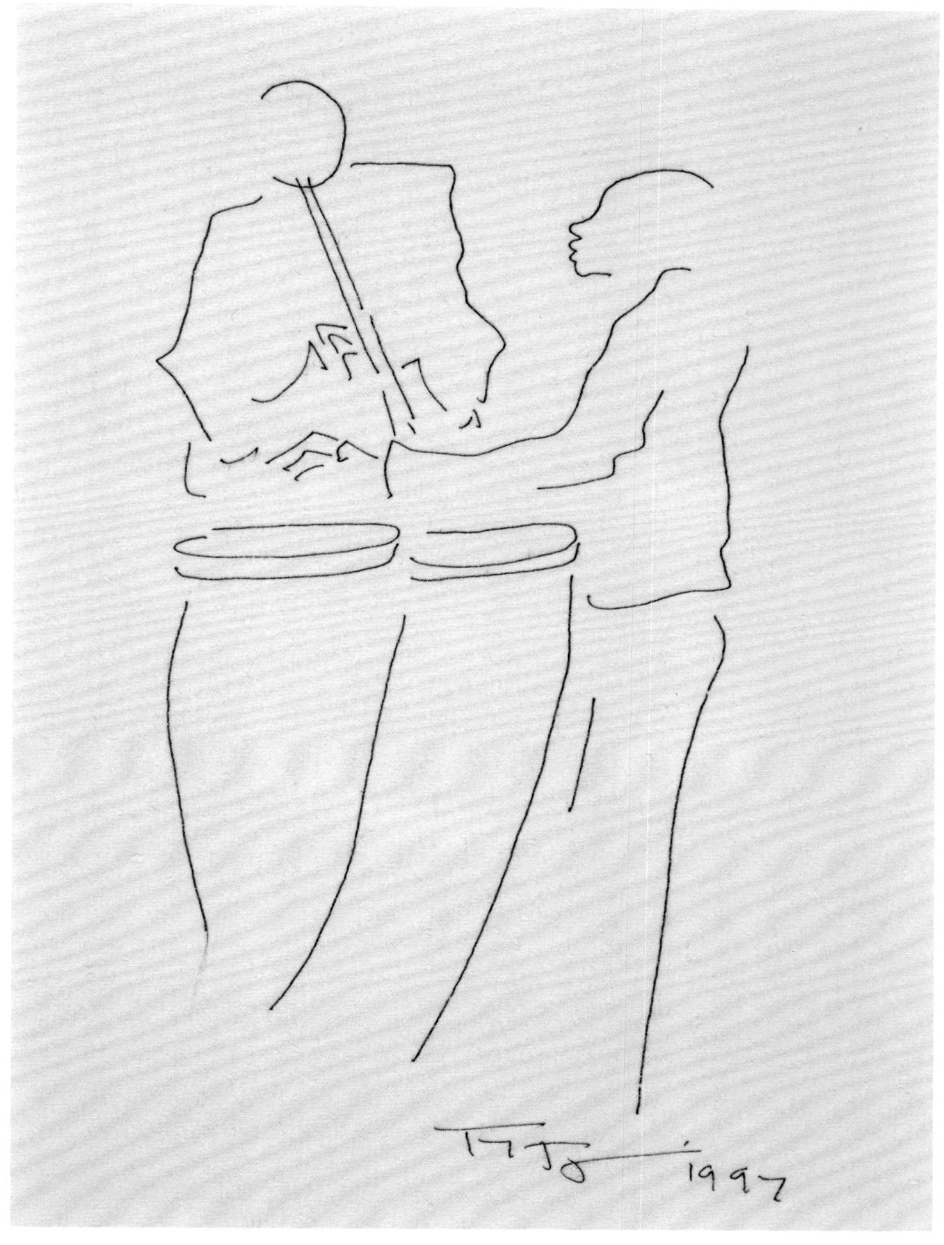

FRANK FRAZIER, Born 1943

Drums for the Nations, 1997, ink on paper, collection of Drs. Willie and Sarah Trotty

REGINALD ADOLPHUS GAMMON, Born 1921

My Family Album, 1972, acrylic and burlap on canvas,
collection of Drs. Russell H. and Rosalind Curry Jackson

Acropolis Girl Olowe, 2005, mixed media on paper, collection of Aleice E. Goodson

KOJO GRIFFIN, Born 1971
Untitled, from the series *Field Theory: group scene,* 2000, mixed media on panel,
the Museum of Fine Arts, Houston, museum purchase

Kojo Griffin uses the charm of imaginative figures, bright colors, and repetitive symbols to pull the viewer into a composition that is based on subject matter that can often be complex and troubling. A psychology major in college who had created art throughout his young life, Griffin strives to elicit a sense of accountability from the viewer. Here, one is confronted with the discomfort of witnessing childlike characters participate in activities that result in negative consequences. While one person may view the three standing figures in this piece as an angry mob that has caused harm to the figure lying helplessly on the ground, another individual may consider them to be good Samaritans coming to his aid.

TRENTON DOYLE HANCOCK, Born 1974

Torpedoboy's Chest Mess, 1999, felt, acrylic, canvas, and found objects, collection of Lester Marks

A Texas native living and working in Houston, Trenton Doyle Hancock had his art exhibited in back-to-back Whitney Biennials, in 2000 and 2002, becoming one of the youngest artists in the history of the biennial to be featured in the prestigious exhibition. Hancock was also a Core Artist in Residence at the Glassell School of Art of the Museum of Fine Arts, Houston, in 2002. Hancock's imaginative work explores the story of "the Mounds," mythical creatures that come to life through his art in drawings, installations, and open-ended mixed-media works.

Egyptian Collar, from the series *The Hoop Dreamin Collection*, 1995, mixed media, collection of Ron and Irene Johnson

Ann Johnson became intrigued with basketball goals as symbols of the genius of black athleticism after viewing a work by Michael Ray Charles, in which he reflects on the dilemma of the African American athlete in a contemporary world of glorification/exploitation. *Egyptian Collar* brings to this piece of sports equipment the adornment of ancient history. Born and reared in Cheyenne, Wyoming, Johnson was influenced by the elaborate beading and adornment that were always a part of the Native American costumes on view at traditional gatherings.

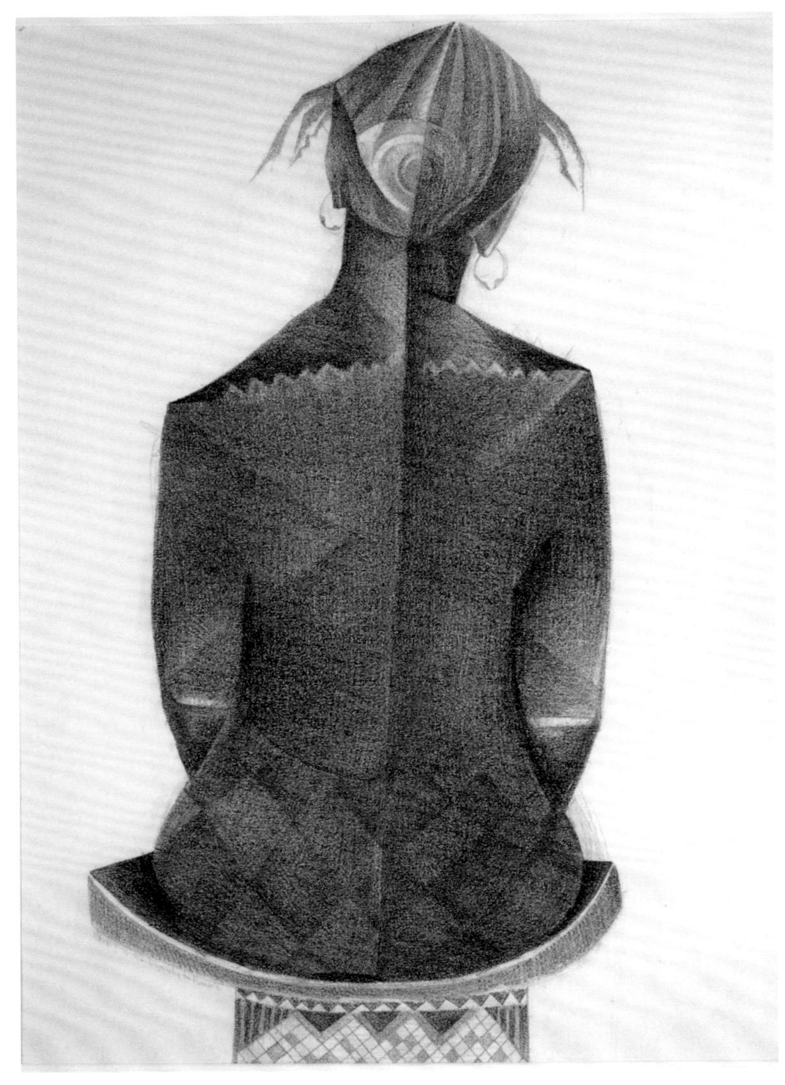

HARVEY L. JOHNSON, Born 1947

God's Trombone, 1982, conté crayon on paper, collection of Florence Jackson-Evans

The Chief, 1990, wood, paint, textile, metal, glass, feather, leather, and a tooth, collection of Wilbert and Sonya Taylor

JEAN LACY, Born 1932

Gift of God Bar, 1976, crayon, ink, and photo-offset printing on collaged elements
on illustration board, the Museum of Fine Arts, Houston, museum purchase
with funds provided by the African American Art Advisory Association

Jean Lacy was born in Washington, D.C., and grew up near the campus of
Howard University. At an early age, she learned of the philosophical
thoughts and writings of Alain Locke, W.E.B. DuBois, and other African
American scholars and activists. This intellectual inquiry has remained with
the artist throughout her life and represents the foundation of her artistic
compositions. Collage offers Lacy the opportunity to combine complex
ideas into a single, albeit multilayered, image.

PARADISE
THE GIFT
GIFT OF GOD BAR

ANNETTE LAWRENCE, Born 1965
Rock Writing, 1992, lava and limestone rocks,
the Museum of Fine Arts, Houston, gift of AT&T,
New Art/New Visions, and the Wilder Foundation

Whether they build on the issues of race, ancestry, or the passage of time, the installations of Annette Lawrence are best known for being elegant constructions that deliberately utilize simple materials like postage string, butcher paper, and cellophane tape. The centerpiece of this lava and limestone installation is a statement that boldly reads, "THEY MUST DON'T KNOW WHO WE ARE." Overheard by the artist while standing in line at a checkout counter, the words became for Lawrence an authentic response of African Americans to a world that often overlooks the importance and complexity of black culture.

THEY
MUST
DON'T
KNOW
WHO
WE
ARE

JESSE LOTT, Born 1943

Black Madonna, c. 1985, wood, collection of Jim and Ann Harithas

BERT L. LONG, JR., Born 1940

Triptych, 1980, acrylic on canvas with mirrors, mounted on galvanized steel, collection of Marilyn Oshman

FLETCHER MACKEY, Born 1950

Jacob's Ladder, c. 1992, wood and metal, collection of Barry and Michelle Barnes

Untitled, 2002–3, charcoal on wood with found knives,
collection of Melanie Lawson and John Guess, Jr.

DELITA PINCHBACK MARTIN, Born 1972

Archetype, 2001, mixed media on paper,
collection of Reginald and Merinda Martin, Jr.

TIERNEY MALONE, Born 1964

Jazz Studies I (Have Swing {Life on the Road}), 1997, tempera, chalk, pastel stick, collage, and marker on paper, the Museum of Fine Arts, Houston, gift of Nina and Michael Zilkha

DAVID MCGEE, Born 1962

Othello, n.d., acrylic on canvas, collection of Karen and Ramon Manning

ANGELBERT METOYER, Born 1977

Father, 2000, mixed media on paper, collection of Lester Marks

Angelbert Metoyer traces his ancestry back to Natchitoches, Louisiana, and his Creole heritage is a central influence on his drawings and paintings. The beauty of his drawings is combined with a fluid application of paint and overlays of symbols and numerical systems, all of which the artist has developed as part of his visual vocabulary.

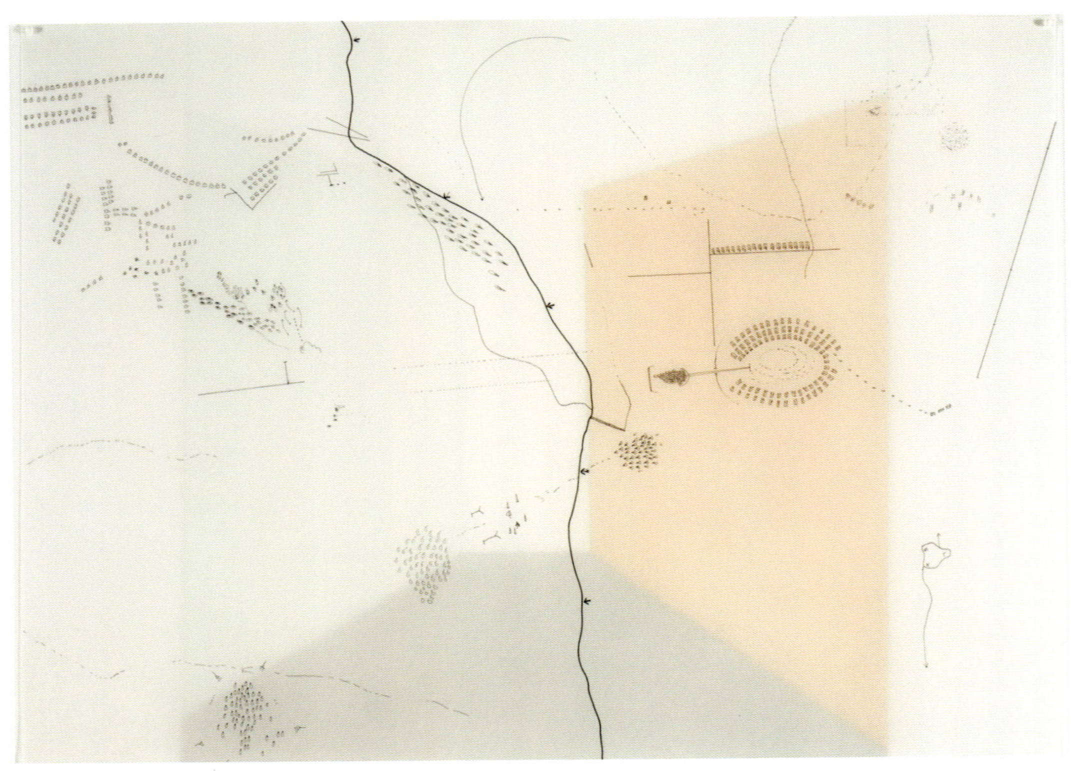

JULIE MEHRETU, Born Ethiopia, 1970

Untitled, 1999, ink on vellum mounted on board, collection of Lester Marks

Born in Ethiopia, Julie Mehretu utilizes the concept of mapping as a visual metaphor for human migration. Her art is visually layered and draws from traditions such as the Italian Futurists, while simultaneously pulling from architectural forms and urban planning maps; these are transformed into a fictional landscape that resonates in today's fast-paced society.

JEFFREY COOK, Born 1961

Wisdom, 2001, mixed media, collection of Michael W. Page

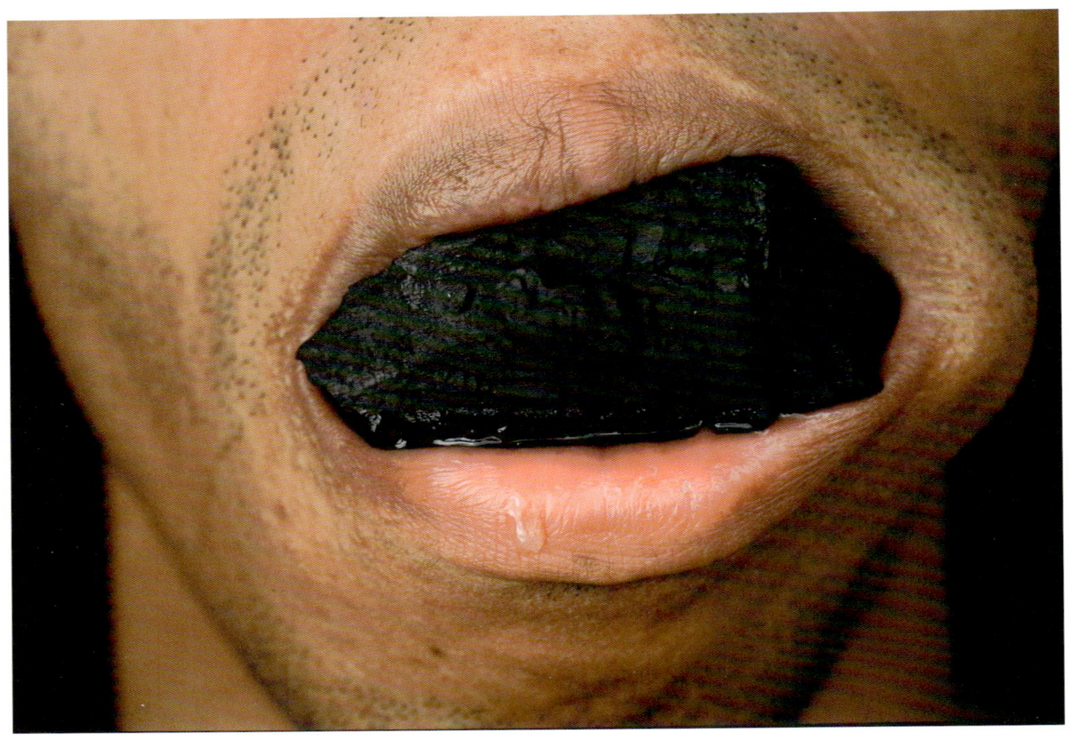

DEMETRIUS OLIVER, Born 1975

Lump, 2005, chromogenic photograph, edition of 10, the Museum of Fine Arts, Houston, gift of Jack Drake

FLOYD NEWSUM, Born 1950

Many Directions, One Path, 2005, mixed media, private collection

ROBERT PRUITT, Born 1975

Elegant Garveyite, 2004, conté crayon on paper, collection of Tina Knowles

KERMIT OLIVER, Born 1943

Beneath Cerements of a Salt Grass Fire, George sits Illumed Against a Flowering Jimsonweed, Pondering Both His Conversation and Promised Sainthood, 1991, acrylic on birch panel, collection of Jan and Jack Cato

ALVIN ROY, Born 1957

The Water Bearers, 2004, oil on canvas, collection of Neos Architects Craig Grassle, AIA, and Patrick F. Pirtle, AAIA

"Nightlights" Necklace, 1989, glass beads, thread, fabric, and leather, the Museum of Fine Arts, Houston, Helen Williams Drutt Collection, gift of the Morgan Foundation in honor of Catherine Asher Morgan

HUGHIE LEE SMITH, 1915–1999

Poet, 1986, oil on canvas, collection of Melanie Lawson and John Guess, Jr.

GEORGE SMITH, Born 1941

Dogon Pyramid, 1990, iron, collection of Patricia Gregory and the late O'Neil Gregory

KANEEM SMITH, Born 1976

Concealment of Deferred Aspiration, n.d., wood and wax, collection of Dr. Gregory L. Shannon and Gregory Shannon II

CARROLL SOCKWELL, 1943–1992

Untitled, n.d., conté crayon on paper, collection of Julie Bakke

Carroll Sockwell was reared in Washington, D.C., and was an active member of the circle of African American artists that included Sam Gilliam and Alma Thomas. Sockwell suffered a difficult and emotionally troubled childhood, and his psychological problems continued into adulthood as he struggled with alcoholism. The artist committed suicide at age forty-nine.

MICHAEL KAHLIL TAYLOR, Born 1979

Huemonic (Untitled), 2008, oil and acrylic on engraved wood,
collection of Dr. Gregory L. Shannon and Gregory Shannon II

HANK WILLIS THOMAS, Born 1976

Priceless #1, from the series *Branded*, c. 2004, chromogenic photograph, the Museum of Fine Arts, Houston, gift of an anonymous donor in honor of Alvia J. Wardlaw

BOB THOMPSON, 1937–1966

Sorrow, 1963, oil on canvas, collection of Melanie Lawson and John Guess, Jr.,

Bob Thompson arrived on the art scene in New York in 1958, and he made ready friendships with the poets, jazz musicians, and writers of the time. During his short career, Thompson produced more than one thousand paintings, and he is known for his expressive figures and landscapes created in bright, bold colors. These works, in turn, reflect his lifelong interest in jazz and his active involvement in the bebop era.

DEBORAH WILLIS, Born 1948

Sisters, 1993, photograph, linen, silk, and fabric, the Museum of Fine Arts,
Houston, gift of an anonymous donor in honor of Alvia Wardlaw

Sweep, 1994, paper mounted on canvas, private collection